Local Government
and Public Service
Reform Initiative

Local Government
Budgeting

Edited by

MIHÁLY HŐGYE

The Fiscal Decentralization Initiative
for Central and Eastern Europe

LOCAL GOVERNMENT AND PUBLIC SERVICE REFORM INITIATIVE
OPEN SOCIETY INSTITUTE

Address
Nádor utca 11.
H-1051 Budapest, Hungary

Mailing address
P.O. Box 519
H-1357 Budapest, Hungary

Telephone
(36-1) 327-3104

Fax
(36-1) 327-3105

E-mail
lgprog@osi.hu

Web Site
http://lgi.osi.hu/

First published in 2002
by Local Government and Public Service Reform Initiative, Open Society Institute Budapest
Studies on Poland and Romania were supported by the Fiscal Decentralization Initiative.
Fiscal Decentralization Initiative is a joint undertaking of the Council of Europe; the Organization for
Economic Co-operation and Development (OECD); the World Bank Institute (WBI); the United States
Agency for International Development (USAID); the Open Society Institute—represented by the
Local Government and Public Service Reform Initiative (OSI/LGI); the Ministry of Interior, Denmark;
and the United Nations Development Program. FDI Secretariat is based in OSI/LGI.

Copies of the book can be ordered by e-mail or post from LGI.
Printed in Budapest, Hungary, November 2002.
Design & Layout by Createch Ltd.

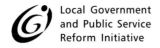 Local Government
and Public Service
Reform Initiative

Local Government and Public Service Reform Initiative (LGI), as one of the programs of the Open Society Institute (OSI), is an international development and grant-giving organization dedicated to the support of good governance in the countries of Central and Eastern Europe (CEE) and the Newly Independent States (NIS). LGI seeks to fulfill its mission through the initiation of research and support of development and operational activities in the fields of decentralization, public policy formation and the reform of public administration.

With projects running in countries covering the region between the Czech Republic and Mongolia, LGI seeks to achieve its objectives through:

- development of sustainable regional networks of institutions and professionals engaged in policy analysis, reform-oriented training and advocacy;
- support and dissemination of in-depth comparative and regionally applicable policy studies tackling local government issues;
- support of country-specific projects and delivery of technical assistance to the implementation agencies;
- assistance to Soros foundations with the development of local government, public administration and/or public policy programs in the countries of the region;
- publication of books, studies and discussion papers dealing with the issues of decentralization, public administration, good governance, public policy and lessons learned from the process of transition in these areas;
- development of curricula and organization of training programs dealing with specific local government issues;
- support of policy centers and think tanks in the region.

Apart from its own projects, LGI works closely with a number of other international organizations (Council of Europe, Department for International Development, USAID, UNDP and the World Bank) and co-funds larger regional initiatives aimed at the support of reforms on the subnational level. The Local Government Information Network (LOGIN) and the Fiscal Decentralization Initiatives (FDI) are two main examples of this cooperation.

For additional information or specific publications, please contact:

Local Government and Public Service Reform Initiative
P.O. Box 519
H–1397 Budapest, Hungary
E-mail: lgprog@osi.hu • http://lgi.osi.hu
Tel: (36-1) 327-3104 • Fax: (36-1) 327-3105

Contents

List of Contributors vii

List of Tables and Figures ix

Preface xiii

PART I.

1. Theoretical Approaches to Public Budgeting 1
   Mihály Hőgye

2. Reform of Budgetary Systems in the Public Sector 17
   Geert Bouckaert

3. Local Government Budgeting: The CEE Experience 43
   Mihály Hőgye • Charles McFerren

   Annex: Terms of Reference 75

   Index 99

PART II.

1. Local Government Budgeting—Albania 103
   Alma Gurraj • Artan Hoxha • Auron Pasha
   Genc Ruli • Qamil Talka • Irma Tanku

2. Local Government Budgeting—Bulgaria 155
   Ginka Tchavdarova • Stefan Ivanov • Emil Savov

3. Local Government Budgeting—Croatia 215
   Katarina Ott • Anto Bajo

4. Local Government Budgeting—Estonia 273
   Georg Sootla ▪ *Annika Jaansoo* ▪ *Paul Tammert*
   Dag Ainsoo ▪ *Eliko Pedastsaar* ▪ *Tarmo Tüür*
   Tähve Milt ▪ *Aivar Surva*

5. Local Government Budgeting—Hungary 329
   Ákos Szalai ▪ *Ferenc Zay* ▪ *Mihály Hőgye*
   Izabella Barati ▪ *Ábel Berczik*

6. Local Government Budgeting—Poland 397
   Jan Filas ▪ *Tony Levitas* ▪ *Marzena Piszczek*

7. Local Government Budgeting—Romania 465
   Afrodita Popa ▪ *Pena Antonevici* ▪ *Victor Gosan*
   Carmen Pop

8. Local Government Budgeting—Russia 521
   A.I. Kuzmin ▪ *E.A. Kachanova* ▪ *I.A. Pykhova*
   S.S. Pushkarev ▪ *D.V. Osintsev*

List of Contributors

Albania
- *Institutes:* Institute for Development Research and Alternatives, and Institute for Contemporary Studies
- *Research team:* Irma Tanku, Auron Pasha, Qamil Talka, Artan Hoxha; Genc Ruli, Alma Gurraj

Bulgaria
- *Institute:* the National Association of Municipalities in the Republic of Bulgaria
- *Research team:* Ginka Tchavdarova, Stefan Ivanov, Emil Savov

Croatia
- *Institute:* Institute of Public Finance
- *Research team:* Katarina Ott, Anto Bajo

Estonia
- *Institute:* Tallinn University of Educational Sciences
- *Research team:* Georg Sootla, Annika Jaansoo, Paul Tammert, Dag Ainsoo, Eliko Pedastsaar, Tarmo Tüür, Tähve Milt, Aivar Surva

Hungary
- *Institute:* Center for Public Affairs Studies Foundation, Budapest University of Economic Sciences and Public Administration
- *Research team:* Ákos Szalai, Mihály Hőgye, György Jenei, Izabella Barati, Ferenc Zay

Poland
- *Institutes:* Levitas Consultants, Ltd., and Krakfin S.C.
- *Research team:* Jan Filas, Tony Levitas, Marzena Piszczek

Romania
- *Institute:* Center of Studies and Programs for Development
- *Research team:* Afrodita Popa, Pena Antonevici, Victor Giosan, Carmen Pop

Russia

- *Institutes:* Ural Academy of Public Administration, Institute of Economy of the Ural branch of the Academy of Sciences of the Russian Federation and the Ural State University
- *Research team:* Alexander I. Kuzmin, Elena A. Kachanova, Iraida A. Pykhova, Sergei S. Pushkarev, D. V. Osintsev

Project Management and Research

- *Institute:* Center for Public Affairs Studies Foundation, Budapest University of Economic Sciences and Public Administration
- *Research team:* Mihály Hőgye, Ákos Szalai, Geert Bouckaert, Charles McFerren, Izabella Barati

List of Tables and Figures

TABLES

PART I.

Table 2.1: Questions for Financial Systems 25
Table 2.2: Focus of Budget and Focus of Change 26
Table 2.3: Input- and Output-Oriented Financial Management Systems:
Comparing Positions 27
Table 2.4: Trajectories of Budget Systems 31
Table 2.5: Accounting Trajectories 33
Table 2.6: Audit Trajectories 34
Table 2.7: Coherence of Some Trajectories
in Budgeting, Accounting and Auditing 36
Table 2.8: Conditions for Success: Global Trajectories 37

Table 3.1: Cash Management 57

PART II.

Table 1.1: Role of Local Government in the Macro-Economy 110
Table 1.2: Total Expenditure by Functions 122
Table 1.3: Revenues of the Municipalities 123
Table 1.4: Revenues from Local Taxes and Fees 123

Table 2.1: Structure of Municipalities 161
Table 2.2: Total Expenditures by Functions, According to the Tiers 165
Table 2.3: Current Revenues of Municipalities 169
Table 2.4: Municipal Current Expenditures by Functions
and Economic Categories, Local Government 174
Table 2.5: Capital Budget in 1999 187
Table 2.6: Actual Budget Performance versus Planned
in 1999 for All Municipalities 192
Table 2.7: Service Expenditure Breakdown,
by Level of Municipal Control in 1998 197

Table 3.1:   Division of Competencies among Levels of Government 225
Table 3.2:   Functional Classification of Expenditure of the Central
              Government, Communes, Cities and Counties in 1999 227
Table 3.3:   Current Expenditures of Local Units in Terms
              of Economic Categories in 1999 229
Table 3.4:   Ratio of Public Debt to GDP in the 1996 to 2000 Period 231
Table 3.5:   Revenue of Local Units in % of Total Budgetary Revenue 232
Table 3.6:   The Structure of Realization of Total Revenue
              by Kind of Unit in 1999 233
Table 3.7:   Main Tax Revenues of Local Units
              as a Percentage of Total Tax Revenue 234
Table 3.8:   Revenues from User Charges and Administrative Fees 235
Table 3.9:   Capital Expenditures and Capital Revenues
              of Local Units in 1999 238

Table 4.1:   Municipalities by Size in 2000 279
Table 4.2:   Current Expenditures by Function and Level of Government,
              1997–1999 282
Table 4.3:   Total Expenditures by Functions in 1999 283
Table 4.4:   The Structure of Current Revenues of Municipalities in 2000 285
Table 4.5:   Number of Municipalities Where Local Taxes Have Been
              Imposed, 1996–1999 287
Table 4.6:   Sources of Investment Funds According to Local
              Community Size (2000) (in %) 295

Table 5.1:   Basic Data on the Size of the Municipalities (1999) 335
Table 5.2:   Total Expenditures by Function, According to the Tiers (1999) 338
Table 5.3:   Municipal Current Expenditures
              by Functions and Cost Type (1996) 340
Table 5.4:   Sources of Municipality Revenues (1998) 343
Table 5.5:   Local Tax Revenues, According to the Autonomy
              of Municipalities (1999) 344
Table 5.6:   The Assessment of the Hungarian Municipal Budgeting
              Techniques Following Meyers' Criteria for Effective Budgeting 387

Table 6.1:   *Gmina* Expenditures in 1999 404
Table 6.2:   County Expenditures in 1999 405
Table 6.3:   Region (Sejmik) Expenditures in 1999 407
Table 6.4:   Shares of Local Government Expenditure in 1999 408

Table 6.5:   Consolidated Public Expenditures
              by Level of Government in 1999 408
Table 6.6:   Organizational Forms of Municipal Utilities
              by Sector: 1995–96 409
Table 6.7:   Revenues of Budgetary Enterprises: 1991–1997 409
Table 6.8:   Budgetary Enterprises and Auxiliary Units in 1999 410
Table 6.9:   Structure of *Gmina* Revenues: 1991–1998 414
Table 6.10:   *Gmina* Investments as a Percentage of Total Revenues
              and GDP: 1994–1999 in PLN 416
Table 6.11:   Revenues of Counties and Regions in 1999 417

Table 7.1:   Responsibilities for the Provision of Public Services 479
Table 7.2:   Macro-Economic Indicators 480
Table 7.3:   Public Expenditures as a % of GDP 480
Table 7.4:   Structure of Local Expenditures in 1999 481
Table 7.5:   Structure of Local Government Revenues in 1999 486

Table 8.1:   Total Expenditures by Functions, in Different Types
              of Municipalities and in the State Budget,
              as a Percentage of the total 535
Table 8.2:   The Structure of Local Budget Revenues and Loans
              in the Russian Federation in 1998 541

FIGURES

PART I.

Figure 2.1:   Policy Cycle—Conceptual Framework 39
Figure 2.2:   Procedural Cycle for Policy and Management 40

Figure 3.1:   Institutional Control Structures 50
Figure 3.2:   Timing Issues 52
Figure 3.3:   Participants in the Decision-Making Process.................................... 55
Figure 3.4:   The Local Government Budget Is Just the Tip of the Iceberg............ 59
Figure 3.5:   A Model for Best Practice Transfer 64

PART II.

Figure 1.1:   The Organizational Structure of Local Governance and the
               Responsibilities of their Respective Bodies 115
Figure 1.2:   Bodies at the Regional Level 116

Figure 4.1:   Institutional Structure of Local Government in Estonia 280

Preface

In summer 2000, the Local Government and Public Service Reform Initiative, which is affiliated with the Open Society Institute Budapest, announced a call for proposals for an international project in the Central and Eastern European transition countries concerning "Local Government Budgeting." The project aimed to identify the critical elements of local budgeting in selected countries and to contribute to local finance and budgeting policy design.

Teams from Central and Eastern Europe and the former Soviet Union region were invited to submit their expressions of interest. Country teams had to demonstrate previous involvement in local government financial issues in the region.

After preliminary discussions, it soon became obvious that a classical international comparative project on local budgeting would be premature. Local basic institutions, legislation, finances and motivation are so diverse in Central and Eastern Europe that no common methodology could be developed for the participants. A joint framework for the regional research would have been very general in order to incorporate all the different local systems in the region, with the probable result being that the findings would not have been satisfactory or useful for any of the participants because of the superficial nature of the comparative information.

However, because of the importance of local budgeting in the countries of the region, a solution had to be found. In the end, various approaches were harmonized by selecting one common topic, while at the same time relying heavily on local initiatives. Each participating country in the regional project was therefore responsible for identifying its relevant problems, under the coordinated research program.

The joint framework of the regional project has been the budgetary policy and process in local government. The studies encompassed the legislative and institutional system of budgeting, thus revealing the relations between central and local budgetary policies. While primarily focusing on local political and administrative processes, various aspects of local budgeting like accounting, information, management, expenditure planning and capital budgeting were analyzed. This general topic provided sufficient autonomy for the members of the research team. At the same time, it was specific enough to connect all the country research projects into a regional whole.

Another purpose of the project has been to encourage the participants to identify the critical components of local budgeting in their own countries. Since organizational and managerial settings of local finances are very diverse in the region, the project's secondary objective was to prioritize the domestic needs. As a result, the in-country research has led to policy advice on these locally selected issues.

Obviously, the parallel work in countries with different traditions and diverse institutions gives an opportunity to compare the outcomes of research. Exchange of information among team members and other countries with similar problems have helped to improve policy design and to provide generalizations of local budgeting practices in the region.

The project was implemented in a coordinated way following a similar approach in selected countries. It has served both the purposes of domestic policy design and exchange of comparative information within the region. The research and development of the project were based on the cooperation of country teams. In this project, participating countries enjoyed great autonomy and flexibility in accomplishing the generally agreed objectives. One expert from the Public Management Center at the Katholieke University of Leuven, Belgium, also provided academic and professional support for the research.

Major steps and stages of the project were the following:

1) *Inviting country teams*

   Project proposals were prepared on a competitive basis by 27 groups of professionals or organizations from 16 countries. The Steering Committee of the Local Government and Public Service Reform Initiative selected teams from eight countries. These were Albania, Bulgaria, Croatia, Estonia, Hungary, Poland, Romania and Russia. The countries represent different types of local government systems (e.g., centralized and more decentralized countries, more and less autonomous local budgeting). Teams from these countries were invited to the preparatory workshop of the project. Country teams had separate contracts and budgets to implement their projects independently.

2) *Preparatory workshop*

   At the first meeting, the representatives of the selected teams discussed the scope of the work and assessed the country needs. The outcome of the preparatory workshop was a clear guideline for designing projects with a focus on country specific issues. Areas of international comparison were identified as well.

3) *Project implementation*

   Country teams implemented the project by doing the following:
   - Elaborating a country study about the budgeting system prevailing at both the central and local levels, with a focus on the relevant legislative and administrative aspects, as well as on the provision of reliable statistics.
   - Doing field research including interviews in local financial departments about targeted issues.
   - Elaborating case studies and good practices.
   - Editing and revising a final report.

4) *Progress reports and evaluating conference*

Country teams had to report the progress as well as financial statements of their project according to their contractual conditions. The final reports as a summary of country study and field research findings were discussed in an evaluating conference with country representatives, advisors and invited experts. These also provided an opportunity for the program manager (LGI and the appointed coordinator) to control the in-country work.

5) *Peer-reviews and editorial work*

After the evaluation conference, independent experts were asked to review and evaluate each country report. On the basis of these peer-reviews, country teams were required to revise their reports and re-submit them to the project manager for final editing prior to publication.

6) *Summary reports, dissemination*

The country reports and studies have been summarized with general lessons for the CEE region. This summary report and the edited outputs of the country researches have been published and disseminated.

Coordination is needed to provide quality control and to support information exchange. An appointed manager supported by some invited experts has been responsible for managing the project under the professional control of LGI. The project manager's roles were to organize the workshop and the conference, to provide supporting materials (terminology, terms of references) to the country teams, to manage any professional discussions with the country teams and to write and publish the summary report for LGI. The manager has worked closely with the LGI in-house research director. Country teams have been working independently according to the goals and conditions set out in their contract with LGI.

The Local Government and Public Service Reform Initiative sponsored the activities of the project management and the research teams of Albania, Croatia, Estonia, Hungary, Poland and Russia. The country studies on Bulgaria and Romania were written with the financial support of the Fiscal Decentralization Initiative for Central and Eastern Europe (FDI–CEE) Program.

The final research report presented here consists of the following parts: Part I is divided into three chapters. Chapter 1 explores theoretical concepts on budgeting as a policy process. Chapter 2 gives an overview and analysis of the modernization and reforms of public budgeting in developed countries. In the comparative approaches to the project (Chapter 3), the authors have attempted to give a general view on the common and different characteristics of local government budgeting in the partner countries. This approach has also allowed the authors to comment on and evaluate some basic features of the systems. The Terms of Reference is attached to this part in order to provide the reader with the common questions that were raised at the start of the research, thus providing a basis for evaluating the results of the research.

Comprehensive country reports are then presented in Part II. The reports on local government budgeting include chapters with almost similar titles in each. Hopefully, it helps the reader to see and compare the elements of the different systems in detail. Each country more or less followed the instructions of the Terms of Reference, while remaining free to emphasize their own most significant issues and problems.

I want to express my profound gratitude to the many people who have supported this project in various ways.

First, I wish to express appreciation to Gábor Péteri, Research Director at the Local Government and Public Service Reform Initiative in Budapest, who has carefully managed this international research. He monitored, encouraged, supported and offered advice on the entire project and even participated in workshops while guiding the project's progress.

My appreciation also extends to the Local Government and Public Service Reform Initiative affiliated with the Open Society Institute, and the Fiscal Decentralization Initiative for Central and Eastern Europe for the essential financial support that made this report possible.

Many thanks for the excellent collaboration with the team managers in the partner countries: Artan Hoxha, Albania; Ginka Tchavdarova, Bulgaria; Katarina Ott, Croatia; Georg Sootla, Estonia; Ákos Szalai, Hungary; Tony Levitas and Marzena Piszczek, Poland; Afrodita Popa, Romania; Alexander Kuzmin, Russia; and to their colleagues in each of the research teams.

A special thanks is extended to the professional advisor in international and comparative approaches, Geert Bouckaert, Belgium, for his valuable assistance.

I also greatly appreciate Charles McFerren's contribution to the comparative approaches and his indispensable copy editorial work.

I also wish to express my appreciation to the experts who have undertaken the difficult job of peer-reviewing: Ardian Dhima, Albania; Alexander Mihaylov, Bulgaria; Helena Blazic, Croatia; Veiko Tammearu, Estonia; Zsuzsanna Kassó, Hungary; Pawel Swianiewicz, Poland; Gábor Kolumbán, Romania; and Elena Nikolaenko, Russia.

Mihály Hőgye
Project Manager
Budapest, Hungary

June 2002

CHAPTER 1

Theoretical Approaches to Public Budgeting

Mihály Hőgye

Table of Contents

Features and Functions of a Public Budget 5

Evolution of a Theory? 8

Rules and Norms for Public Budgeting 9

Notes 13

References 14

Theoretical Approaches to Public Budgeting

Mihály Hőgye

FEATURES AND FUNCTIONS OF A PUBLIC BUDGET

A significant development in the intellectual history of the 20th century has been the explicit recognition by economists, politicians and the public at large of the importance of government in the operation of the economy.[1] The public budget generally reflects the policy of the government toward the economy.[2] Public budget is a forecast of governmental expenditures and revenues for the ensuing fiscal year, which may or may not correspond to the calendar year. Except for primitive economies, the budget is the key instrument for the expression and execution of government economic policy. Public budgets have wide implications for the national economy. By budgets governments exercise their allocative, stabilization and distributive functions.[3] They are, therefore, political as well as economic documents and are products of the political processes by which competing interests in any nation achieve agreement.

Although the major budgetary decisions that effect the performance of the economy and the national debt are usually made by the central government, most countries have local or state (provincial) governments. These are responsible for the provision of various services and have the authority to raise revenues through taxation or to borrow on their own account. This devolution of authority is greatest in the United States, where the majority of provision of civilian services is carried out at state or local levels and where states have a tradition of being individual decision-making units. In the United Kingdom, by contrast, local authority spending is constrained by rules set by the central government. Local authorities are also limited in their ability to borrow and to raise taxes, which are set by the central government. (The budget of the European Union is an example where authority for major spending, particularly for agricultural support, has devolved to a transnational body.)

The difficulty of discussing *budgeting as a policy process* lies basically in the difference between discussing private sector companies or individuals and government budgeting. Although the process of preparing and discussing a public budget has progressed considerably during the 20th century, it is in a number of senses still inferior to the way budgeting is carried out by private sector companies or indeed by individuals. Commercial practice is governed by a series of well-defined rules, and firms are required to produce a balance sheet, a profit and loss account and to monitor their cash flow carefully. The total indebtedness of a company is monitored closely by its shareholders, who are also critical of future forecasts of profits and growth. Individuals who fail to budget adequately are equally closely monitored by bank managers and credit agencies, and those with complicated affairs can draw upon skilled professional help.

The *accountability of government*, even in a well-developed democracy, is in reality considerably less acute, or certainly less clear, than that of companies to their shareholders or individuals to their various creditors. As a result, public budgeting is frequently of lower quality than is the norm in the private sector. Forecasts of receipts and expenditures are often wildly at variance with reality; changes to accounting practices are sometimes made for cosmetic political purposes and certain distinctions, such as those between capital and current expenditures, are frequently blurred deliberately. These criticisms of the public budgetary process are more valid in some countries than in others.

According to Aronson and Schwartz (1981) the extent of the budget amounts and the operating programs on which they are based is the dividing line between the private and the public sectors. The budget stipulates which goods and services are to be supplied to the public by the authorities and which are to be supplied by the private sector. The decision on who is to supply what and who is to receive what should be a reflection of the community's values, preferences and priorities. Therefore, the budget is a political document through which money is appropriated according to value judgments and the budget process is a political process that takes place within a political arena (Gildenhuys, 1997).

Thornhill (1984) summarizes the most important features of a public budget as follows:[4]

- The budget, after its approval by the legislative authority, is enforceable.
- The results of most of the objectives to be realized by the budget are not quantifiable.
- The budget brings together a variety of considerations.
- As the objectives of action taken by public institution differ widely from those of private organizations, the processes for determining the content of a public budget are therefore unique.
- Authorities do not always adapt their expenditure to fit their available revenue.

It may therefore be stated that a public budget is an instrument at the disposal of the legislative authority. It enables to guide the economic, social, political and other activities of a community in a certain direction in order to realize predetermined goals and objectives, the results of which are not always quantifiable. The budget also contains all of the measures needed to subordinate the executive authority to the legislative authority as the representative of the voters and taxpayers. The features of a public budget ensure the unique foundation on which its preparation, approval and execution are based. In public administration the budget serves as a decision-making instrument by which priorities are set, goals and objective are established, operating programs are compiled and control exercised. A budget document is the final product in the budget process and it should be suitable for consideration and approval by the legislative authority, while the execution of its contents should realize public objectives. The quality of the budget depends on the accuracy of the supporting data, the quality of the methods used and the expertise as well as the integrity with which it has been compiled. As a result of the broad spectrum of services that an authority has to render, however, budgets can offer only a synoptic picture of their financial implications. Therefore, a compromise has to be made in the budget document between the requirements for adequate, accurate information and for manageability (Kotzé, 1979).[5]

Gildenhuys (1997) recognizes the functions of a pubic budget as follows:

- The budget is a policy statement declaring the goals and specific objectives an authority wishes to achieve by means of the expenditure concerned. It is public policy expressed in amounts of money and is the actual embodiment of policy and of implied policy objective. In policy-making, realization of the most important objectives and aims should receive priority. As a policy-making document, the budget generally contains a definition of both the quantity and the quality of the envisaged service delivery. However, no normative guidelines exist by which priorities may be scientifically determined, thus that is the result of political expedience.

- The redistribution of wealth is one of the most important functions of a public budget. It requires that total integration should exist between the two sides of the budget—revenue policy and expenditure policy—in order to comply with a fiscal policy for the redistribution of wealth.

- For the administrative authority, the budget is a work program on which each department can base its own operational work program. This function of the budget demands that the structure of objectives, the activity schedule, the resource schedule and the financial schedule is clearly expounded in the budget documents.

- The budget serves as a source of information for everyone concerned; the information contained in the draft budget document is necessary for its consideration and, after approval, serves as the most important source of information to the administrative authority for executing its functions.

- The budget also serves as a coordinating instrument by which government activities can be integrated, because it is supposed to contain all the information on the policies, objectives and activities of the government in one document.

- The budget is also a control instrument to be used by the legislative authority over the executive authority and by the executive authority over the administrative authority and even for internal control within a single component of the administrative authority. Two types of administration control are important in this regard, namely, *a priori* control and *ex post* control.

EVOLUTION OF A THEORY?

The applicability of the word "theory" in this area is a far cry from its usage in the social sciences, particularly in economics. This has been explicitly recognized by the quasi patron saint in the field, Wildavsky, who said: "...a normative theory of budgeting would be a comprehensive and specific political theory detailing what the government's action ought to be at a particular time. Given that the budget represents the outcome of political struggle, a normative theory of budgeting suggests the elimination of any such conflict over the government's role in society. Such a theory, therefore, is utopian in the fullest sense of the word: Its creation and acceptance would mean the end of politics."[6]

Much of the literature on public budgeting emanates from the United States, where in the 1960s "incrementalism" became the dominant theory of budgeting. Incrementalism is a style of policy-making based on small, marginal changes from existing policies. It contends not only that comprehensive rationality is impossible, but also that policies are seldom changed radically as a result of extensive reviews.[7] It is a tendency of government to tinker with policies rather than to question the value of continuing them. Considering the work of Wildavsky (1964), Fenno (1965) and others, budget processes were seen as stable, predictable, changing little from year to year and based on well defined roles that could be represented by relatively simple decision rules. They argue that a process which concentrates on an increment is preferable to one that attempts to review the whole budget because it moderates conflict, reduces search costs, stabilizes budgetary roles and expectations, and reduces the amount of time that officials must invest in budgeting, thus increasing the likelihood that important political values will be taken into account. The term incrementalism promises budgetary growth within most of the program and expenditure increases. Statistical analysis of incremental outcomes typically measures the amounts and rates of increase. Descriptive studies concentrate on the tactics used to augment the basic in "small steps." However, incrementalism offers little explanation as to how decisions are made or how the increment is divided (Schick, 1983).

By the late 1970s incrementalism was seriously challenged as a theory of budgeting (LeLoup, 1978) because of the narrowness of its analytical focus and changes in the environment and processes of budgeting. "When a theory applies to all situations at all times without the possibility of disconfirming evidence, it is no longer a theory and of little use for explanation or even description."[8]

As economic and social intervention by governments has increased, the limitations of incrementalism as a budgeting practice have become increasingly apparent. A number of techniques or attempts to reforming budget systems have been introduced to make decisions more rational. These techniques have been applied with different speeds by local and regional governments as well.

Evolution of budget theory and policy-making shows that undeniable progress has been achieved, often on modest fronts and with reasonably simple techniques. A key development in budget theory has been the differentiation between *microbudgeting and macrobudgeting* and the inherent tension between them (LeLoup, 1988). "Macrobudgeting —high level decisions on spending, revenue and deficit aggregates and relative budget share, often made from top to down. Microbudgeting—intermediate level decisions on agencies, programs, and line-items, usually made from the bottom up."[9] Both levels of analysis are interested in how power is structured in budgetary processes as well as being exercised and expressed through budgetary choices. "The basic conceptualization of budgeting has shifted from a cycle of micro-level, incremental executive requests and legislative actions to a complex series of political responses to short-term economic changes and projections of relatively inflexible long-term trends in outlays and revenues. Key questions now concern how to balance micro-decisions within macro-level parameters. *No grand theory of budgeting has emerged*, but we are closer to explaining the budgetary process...."[10]

RULES AND NORMS FOR PUBLIC BUDGETING

The recent experience of budgeting and policy-making has left behind a substantial body of rules, norms and practices, which are routinely applied or pursued in most countries, because they are widely recognized as workable and reasonably efficient and are required by international organizations and/or financial markets (Lacasse, 1996). Budget norms are explicitly formulated; their compliance or non-compliance is easily observable and, often sanctioned by financial markets.

Mikesell (1991) has also stated that new budget reform techniques are consistent with the classical principles for appraising budgets.[11]

1) *Comprehensiveness.* The budget should include all receipts and outlays of the government. The single process would thus include all activities of the government.

2) *Unity.* All spending and revenue-collecting parts should be related to each other. Consistent evaluation criteria should be applied to any expenditure, regardless of the government area in which it is located.

3) *Exclusiveness.* Only financial matters should be in the budget. (Modern analysts recognize, however, that almost every governmental action has financial implications.)

4) *Specification.* The budget should be executed as it is enacted. Cavalier changes should not be made during the budget year.

5) *Annuality.* The budget should be prepared every year for the next year of agency existence.

6. *Accuracy.* Forecasts should be as reasonable as possible and the document should be internally consistent.
7. *Clarity.* The budget should describe what is proposed in understandable fashion. The document, in an effort to encompass all, should not bury policy intent in line-item detail.
8. *Publicity.* The budget in a representative democracy should not be secret. The budget contains the expenditure plan (as well as the revenue estimates) of the government. It is clearly contrary to the underlying principles of a democracy that such important choices are made without complete public consideration.

According to Lacasse (1996), the three most important budget related rules are: *comprehensiveness* and a *multi-year perspective* in budget elaboration, and the capability for *monitoring implementation* so as to further *accountability* and timely adjustments. (The two latter partly correspond with specification, clarity and publicity.) These issues in budget office-center relations all fall under the three categories of harmonization, complementarity and co-responsibility, as discussed above.

On the other hand, Wildavsky and Caiden (1997), argue that to understand what was happened to budgeting in our time consider the radical changes in the norms of desirable behavior that used to guide budgeters. According to them, budgets emerged at the beginning of the nineteenth century as the result of reforms that replaced centuries of muddle and mismanagement with expenditure control based on norms of annularity, comprehensiveness, legislative appropriation, audit and balance. Public budgets today are evaluated against their *long-term implications*, they consist of many different kinds of spending, and they are unbalanced, uncertain and dependent on circumstances beyond their control.

As far as the norm of *comprehensiveness* concerns, the rule could be rewritten as: every penny whose allocation is made via the political process, not the market, should be recorded and presented for assessment in the budget. Very little dispute has arisen around this rule at the theoretical level, however, in practice this is a much more demanding rule. This rule has been broken by direct loans, loan guarantees, tax preferences, off-budget companies, open-ended entitlements and other devices (Wildavsky and Caiden, 1997).

For instance, over the last two decades, the reintegration of special funds into a "normal" budgetary perspective has been one of the biggest changes in implementing this rule. There is also an increasing tendency to treat commercial activities carried by departments and public enterprises for what they are—in other words, the distinctions between commercial and public policy functions have been sharpened. (Privatization has helped on this front.)

Other categories like tax expenditures, guaranties and regulations are not likely to be overcome soon. Implicit guaranties, such as unfunded pension obligations or guaranties to the banking and financial system institutions remain outside the budgetary purview. It is not even clear how they could be included. As well, debate is still going on the very legitimacy of the concept of tax expenditures. The attempts to design and use a regulatory budget have also failed. On the other hand, one can argue that tidying these "loose ends" up might increase the complexity of the budget to such a degree, that it could defeat its very objective of improving transparency and accountability (Lacasse, 1996).

The issue between budgeting and policy-making is more than a straightforward problem of disharmony. The key to the solution—that is to the continuation of the last decades' evolution towards really comprehensive budgets—probably lies in rigorous budgetary laws and rules.

Apart from the temptations to go off-budget, the other important issues seem linked to the choices between regulations and expenditures or between direct expenditures and tax expenditures. Budgeting of tax expenditures, even in a primitive fashion, is rare, while regulatory budgeting has not traveled far from the textbooks and amounts to little more than good intentions (Lacasse, 1996).

The chronological counterpart of the comprehensiveness rule is the *annuality* versus *multi-year budgeting*. The latter demands to reconcile the annual budget with multi-year policy commitments. This apparently contradictory injunction is important in two respects: for new or reformed policies, and for the cross-impacts of policies. In both cases, the elaboration of the current budget demands accurate cost forecasts.

The consensus over the fact that the budget office is a key instrument of control and should play an important role in supplying implementation feedback—indeed, in controlling implementation—is as strong as it is traditional and vague. This somewhat paradoxical situation has a variety of sources. First, institutions vary markedly between countries. Second, the very content of "implementation feedback" is a mixed-bag, ranging from compliance and integrity controls to impact evaluations. Third, basic strategies as to who should be responsible for providing such feedback to whom also vary from country to country, and substantial overlap in responsibilities exists between institutions within countries.

It is assumed that the implementation of the budget routinely and rapidly generates information as to whether the monies voted are indeed being spent within the legislated framework provided by the budget. Such implementation monitoring exists in most countries, but this basic feedback on policy implementation is often limited to financial information and is used almost exclusively by the budget office. This is rarely felt to be enough by the policy-making center, whose attention is obviously oriented towards the future, towards new policies or revised ones (Lacasse, 1996). This is the reason why analysts state that the *control of spending* has declined along with the norm of comprehensiveness (Wildavsky and Caiden, 1997).

The important issues of implementation are related to the systems, institutions and methods aimed at answering simple and age-old questions such as: Is the money being spent efficiently? Is the money reaching those for whom it was intended? Is the policy having the intended results? Is the policy generating unwanted and undesirable effects?

The most difficult and controversial subject addressed by the above questions— namely, whether policies have had the expected impact on society and at a reasonable cost—curiously attracts the strongest consensus.

The subject of efficiency in public management—i.e., of maximizing productivity and minimizing costs in delivering existing policies—is a very political subject in which many budget offices have played a key role in the last decade, essentially as promoters of the so-called "new public management," a concept incorporating business management styles and practices into the public sector. This reform is based on the conjunction of two elements: first, the delegation of financial authority to lower level—including in some cases virtually all aspects of personnel policy, flexibility as to the timing of expenditures, permission to substitute capital for labor and vice-versa—and, second, the introduction of performance commitments and incentives, appropriately backed up by performance measurements and sufficient power at the center to ensure accountability and control. It should be noted however that this evolution is far from being uniform among countries. (See next chapter.)

That the budget should further accountability and provide a key instrument of transparency on government action, is such a staple of budget theory that it has acquired a quasi-theological aura. Nobody is against virtue. However, the practical meaning of this principle has often remained obscure (Lacasse, 1996). The instruments used to make the budget choices and their implementation transparent differ widely from country to country. There is not any unique system likely to be applicable to all countries.

Other phenomena that used to be confined mainly to poor countries—repetitive budgeting, remaking the budget several times a year—have now become standard practices in relatively rich nations as well (Wildavsky and Caiden, 1997).

Why did the norms erode? Answering this question is not easy. The old Politics of the Budgetary Process (Wildavsky) could focus on incremental differences because the base was largely agreed. When there is a disagreement about the starting point as well as the desirable outcome of budgetary negotiation, incremental change is in trouble. Schick (1988) holds another view: prosperity declined, incrementalism has gone with it. Both budgetary norms and spending practices change together. The purpose of norms is to justify practices. The importance of budgetary norms can be seen indirectly in new practices and proposals for reform (budget resolutions, constitutional spending limits, etc.)

NOTES

1   Issues discussed here relate to any level of government existing in a system.

2   A distinction should be made between a budget and a budget system. Whereas the *budget* refers only to the documents within which financial proposals are contained, the *budget system* refers to the relationship between the stages to be followed in order to compile the budget documents (Thornhill, 1984).

3   For a comprehensive description of these functions, see Musgrave, Richard A.: *The Theory of Public Finance*, (New York: McGraw-Hill, 1959).

4   in Gildenhuys, 1997, p.394.

5   in Gildenhuys, 1997, p.395.

6   Wildavsky, Aaron and Naomi Caiden: *The New Politics of the Budgetary Process*, Third edition, (Addison Wesley Longman, Inc., 1997), p.265.

7   Comprehensive rationality is a style of policy-making based on scientific assessment of alternative actions and conscious choice of the course of action that will yield the maximum benefit. It suggests that policies are subjected to multi-step analyses before a decision is made.

8   LeLoup, Lance T.: "The Myth of Incrementalism: Analytical Choices in Budgetary Theory," Reprinted from *Polity*, Vol. X, No. 4, summer 1978, p.502.

9   LeLoup, Lance T.: "From Microbudgeting to Macrobudgeting: Evolution in Theory and Practice," in: Rubin, Irene (ed.): *New Directions in Budget Theory*, (State University of New York, 1988), p.19.

10 p.36.

11 Howard, S. Kenneth: *Changing State Budgeting*, (Lexington, Ky.: Council of State Governments, 1973), pp.5–8. Quoted by J. Mikesell (1991) p.121.

REFERENCES

Aaron Wildavsky: *The Politics of the Budgetary Process*, (Boston: Little Brown, 1964).

Aaron Wildavsky and Naomi Caiden: *The New Politics of the Budgetary Process*, Third edition, (Addison Wesley Longman, Inc., 1997).

Allen Schick: *The Federal Budget, Politics, Policy, Process*, (Washington, DC: The Brookings Institution, 1995).

Allen Schick: *The Capacity to Budget*, (Washington, DC: The Urban Institute Press, 1990).

Allen Schick: "Macro-Budgetary Adaptations to Fiscal Stress in Industrialized Democracies", *Public Administration Review*, Vol. 46, March/April, 1986.

Aronson, J.R. and Eli Schwartz, (eds.): *Management Policies in Local Government Finance*, (Washington DC International City Management Association, 1981).

Axelrod, Donald: *Budgeting for Modern Government*, (New York: St. Martin's Press, 1988).

Axelrod, Donald: *A Budget Quartet, Critical Policy & Management Issues*, (New York: St. Martin's Press, 1989).

Bozeman, Barry and Jeffrey D. Straussman: "Shrinking Budgets and the Shrinkage of Budget Theory," *Public Administration Review*, Vol. 42, November/December, 1982.

Buchanan, James M.: *Public Finance in Democratic Process, Fiscal Institutions and Individual Choice*, (The University of North Carolina Press, 1987).

"Budgeting in Hungary During the Democratic Transition," co-authors: L. LeLoup, A. Dietz, Z. Pápai, L. Urbán and L. Váradi, *Journal of Public Budgeting, Accounting and Financial Management*, Vol. 10, Number 1, Spring 1998.

Fenno, Richard F., Jr.: *The Power of the Purse: Appropriation Politics in Congress*, (Boston: Little Brown, 1966).

Gildenhuys, J.S.H.: *Public Financial Management*, Second edition, (Pretoria: J.L. van Schaik Publishers, 1997).

Gosling, James J.: *Budgetary Politics in American Governments*, (Longman Publishing Group, 1992).

Kowalcky, Linda K. and Lance T. LeLoup: "Congress and the Politics of Statutory Debt Limitation," *Public Administration Review*, Vol. 53, January/February, 1993.

Lacasse, Francois: "Budget and Policy Making: Issues, Tensions and Solutions," in *Budgeting and Policy Making*, (Paris: Sigma Papers: No. 8, 1996).

LeLoup, Lance T.: "The Myth of Incrementalism: Analytical Choices in Budgetary Theory," Reprinted from *Polity*, Vol. X, No. 4, Summer 1978.

LeLoup, Lance T. (ed.): "Appropriations Politics in Congress: The House Appropriations Committee and the Executive Agencies," *Public Budgeting & Finance*, Winter, 1984.

LeLoup, Lance T., Barbara Luck Graham and Stacey Barwick: "Deficit Politics and Constitutional Government: The Impact of Gramm-Rudman-Hollings," *Public Budgeting & Finance*, Spring, 1987.

LeLoup, Lance T.: *Budgetary Politics*, Fourth edition, 1988.

LeLoup, Lance T.: "From Microbudgeting to Macrobudgeting: Evolution in Theory and Practice," in Irene Rubin (ed.), *New Directions in Budget Theory*, (New York: State University of New York, 1988).

LeLoup, Lance T. and Steven A. Shull: *Congress and the President, The Policy Connection*, (Belmont, California: Wadsworth Publishing Company, 1993).

Lynch, Thomas D.: *Public Budgeting in America*, (Englewod Cliffs, N.J.: Prentice-Hall, Inc., 1979).

Lynch, Thomas D.: *Federal Budget & Financial Management Reform*, (Westport: Quorum Books, 1991).

Lynch, Thomas D. and Lawrence L. Martin, (eds.): *Handbook of Comparative Public Budgeting and Financial Management*, (New York: Marcel Dekker, Inc., 1993).

Mikesell, John L.: *Fiscal Administration—Analysis and Applications for the Public Sector*, (Pacific Grove, California: Brooks/Cole Publishing Company, 1991).

Reed, B.J. and John W. Swain: *Public Finance Administration*, Second edition, (Thousand Oaks, California: SAGE Publications Ltd., 1997).

Rubin, Irene (ed.): *New Directions in Budget Theory*, (New York: State University of New York, 1988).

Shuman, Howard E.: *Politics and the Budget, The Struggle Between the President and the Congress*, (Englewod Cliffs, N.J.: Prentice-Hall, Inc., 1992).

Van Reeth, Wouter: *The Search for Meaningful Budgeting*, EGPA Conference paper, (Budapest, 1996).

CHAPTER 2

Reform of Budgetary Systems in the Public Sector

Geert Bouckaert

Table of Contents

1. Trajectories of Modernization 21
    1.1 Partial Trajectories: What, How, When and their Rhetoric 22
    1.2 Consolidating Partial Trajectories into Global Trajectories:
         Internal and External Coherence 23
    1.3 Methodological Problems in Describing Trajectories 23

2. The Financial Management Trajectory 24
    2.1 Budgeting, Financial Management and Performance 24
    2.2 Explaining Modernization of Financial Management 27
    2.3 The Budget Trajectory 29
    2.4 The Accounting Trajectory 32
    2.5 The Audit System 33
    2.6 Generators of Change 35

3. Lessons and Priorities for Transition Countries 36
    3.1 Consolidated Financial Trajectories
         Could Be Facilitated by Having Common Objectives 36
         3.1.1 The Stability and Resource Allocation Trajectory 37
         3.1.2 The Performance Trajectory 38
         3.1.3 The Accountability Trajectory 38
    3.2 A Common Conceptual and Procedural Framework
         Would Support a Sustainable Financial Management 38

References 41

List of Tables and Figures

Table 2.1: Questions for Financial Systems 25

Table 2.2: Focus of Budget and Focus of Change 26

Table 2.3: Input- and Output-Oriented Financial Management Systems:
Comparing Positions 27

Table 2.4: Trajectories of Budget Systems 31

Table 2.5: Accounting Trajectories 33

Table 2.6: Audit Trajectories 34

Table 2.7: Coherence of Some Trajectories
in Budgeting, Accounting and Auditing 36

Table 2.8: Conditions for Success: Global Trajectories 37

Figure 2.1: Policy Cycle—Conceptual Framework... 39

Figure 2.2: Procedural Cycle for Policy and Management 40

Reform of Budgetary Systems in the Public Sector

Geert Bouckaert

1. TRAJECTORIES OF MODERNIZATION

A scenario for modernization and reform could be defined as a description of a present (administrative and political) situation, of possible and desirable future situations and a series of events and decisions that may lead to a particular situation. This implies that three elements are available: a description of the initial situation, a relatively precise idea of a future situation and a causal chain of events that result in this future situation. Scenarios should be used and developed in an *ex ante* situation.

This chapter is about the factual trajectories of some developed countries and not about scenarios or omegas. Practice seems to show that well developed scenarios are rare, and that in some cases limited trajectories exist that are extended in a pragmatic way into chains of trajectories. The next part of a chain of events is in many cases an adjustment to a previous or concurrent partial trajectory.

Therefore, a comparison of trajectories should take into account the alpha position and the expressed omega position. The alpha positions are not fully comparable. The Swedish and Finnish historical tradition of independent agencies and the constitutional protection of their independence are totally different from the newly created Next Steps Agencies in the UK, or the volatile restructuring of ministries in Australia and New Zealand. Depending on divisions of power (majoritarian vs. coalitions), division of responsibilities between competences (finance, personnel, institutions) and levels of government (decentralized, federalized vs. centralized), different starting positions are taken (Pollitt and Bouckaert, 2000).

The omega positions are not made explicit. However some intermediate positions are expressed as intermediate objectives, e.g., agentification or integrating performance related pay.

This makes a comparison of trajectories a challenge. However, the similarity of economic pressures results in focusing on a limited volume of the public sector, on key tasks of administrations and in an awareness of the importance of a well performing public sector for the economy. There also seems to be an increasing convergence of political opinions in the field of modernization. Socialists in Australia and Conservatives in the UK were aiming at similar objectives. This results in taking comparable measures and in observing similar objectives in a contingent environment. Trajectories, sometimes partial ones, should therefore be looked at.

1.1 Partial Trajectories: What, How, When and their Rhetoric

Partial trajectories may refer to parts of the chain in terms of time and number of steps taken, e.g., from mega departments to clusters of agencies. Partial also means that there is a focus on one part of a concurrent and/or simultaneous set of tracks of trajectories. In this chapter there will be an emphasis on the content of the financial trajectory, in a context of trajectories of personnel, organization and performance information systems. This is the what-part of trajectories.

Also the tactics, the way of implementation and the process, is important. This is the how-part of trajectories which may change over time. Political top-down approaches, e.g., in New Zealand are different from institutionalized (guided) bottom-up initiatives in Scandinavia. Yet, the necessity of increasing ownership to enhance success of change may require a shift to encouraging bottom-up approaches. On the other hand, the necessity to focus on savings for a period of time may require (temporarily) shifts to certain patterns of top-down approaches, as in Canada, or of "guided" bottom-up, e.g., frame budgeting, in Sweden and Finland.

These partial trajectories start at a certain moment of time and could be linked and consolidated in chains (time) and coherent clusters (functional). This is the when-part of trajectories that differs immensely. There are early birds (New Zealand and the UK) and there are late bloomers (France and the European Union). There are the different timings of the content parts of the trajectories, e.g., first organization, then personnel and finance and finally information systems. Especially the sequence of different pieces of legislation may be important here. Also the timing of the "awakening" of institutions is important. The finance departments, except, perhaps, the budget part, always seem to have been active. The position of Supreme Audit Offices differs, mostly according to the position of parliament itself. This results in "Push and Pull" trajectories.

Finally, there is the trajectory of rhetoric. There are three dimensions in the country trajectories of rhetoric. First, there is a weak/strong dimension. Leaving the modernization processes endemic (Germany) or invisible (Denmark), or making them visible by just communicating them (France and Finland), or lifting them up by expressing self-fulfilling prophesies which fit in a broader strategy of enhancing leadership legitimacy (USA, UK and New Zealand) is a full scale. Second, there is the content of the rhetoric which may vary from just minimizing the state to modernizing the state in redistributing activity competencies in society between market, hierarchy and citizen participation. Third, there is the political rhetoric (announcing the initiative) and the technical one (on implementation).

1.2 Consolidating Partial Trajectories into Global Trajectories: Internal and External Coherence

These partial trajectories could be consolidated in global ones. The acid test consists of three elements. First, looking at time consolidation of the trajectory (continuity vs. discontinuity; smooth progress vs. shocks; consistent direction of change vs. Copernican changes in policies; small vs. strong variance around the trend). For example, New Zealand and the UK have had a constant policy since the end of the 1980s. Denmark changed from an internal improvement strategy to a market focus after the elections that changed the majority.

Second, what is the functional consolidation of the trajectory (organization, personnel, finance and information) and the convergence and coherence of these different functional dimensions in the concurrent trajectories? There is a question of coherence and convergence inside a functional domain. For example, the European Union seems to trigger initiatives in the fields of evaluation and finance (Fiche Financière) but seems not to change the budget format which consists of two separate parts A and B, which are not related. There is also the question of the integration of the different functional fields. For example, almost all countries consider the integration of performance related information in the policy cycle as a major weakness and difficulty.

Third, what is the tactics-strategy consolidation of the trajectory, or the degree of fit between the tactics of implementation and process on the one hand, and the objectives and systemic features on the other hand? It is not realistic to develop a savings (stability and resource allocation) strategy through a bottom-up approach. The necessity to guarantee savings in Finland and Sweden with its tradition of strong and independent agencies was not possible through a bottom-up approach. A government steered frame budgeting stated the input border lines within which performance management became possible and was facilitated. On the other hand, in Canada, the same top-down process disrupted the bottom-up performance strategy. The implicit theory and model derived hypothesis is that a coherent consolidation enhances the sustainability of the change.

1.3 Methodological Problems in Describing Trajectories

Developing a multiple case study with countries as cases in order to distil trajectories and differences of trajectories is not obvious from a methodological point of view. Apart from the choice of the countries, which is not random, and the time dimension for analysis and assessment, which could make it difficult to observe changes in "results," there are some other significant problems.

There is a problem in disentangling "facts" and "rhetoric." A factual trajectory of shifting to cost accounting is different from the evolving practice of applying this cost accounting and from the rhetoric on the existence and use of cost accounting generated information. Secondary data (mostly developed by those involved in the process) does not always provide a good picture on the relations between decisions, the quality of implementations of decisions and the rhetorical use of this.

Second, foreign languages force researchers to look at translated materials. In many cases, only summaries of best practices are available. The best databases and overviews, e.g., those of the OECD, are not really audited and depend on the assessment of the member countries themselves. This results in an inequilibrated offer of materials which may give an impression of dominance of a particular country or cluster of countries, e.g., the Anglo-Saxon and Westminster countries.

Third, "facts" are not always a one dimensional story. The same event or trajectory, e.g., performance-based contract management, may result in different visions in reality depending on whether one belongs to an agency, a parent ministry, the finance ministry or the supreme audit office. These kaleidoscopic stories of trajectories are not always compatible and complicate the reduction of complexity of changing realities.

Fourth, since there are simultaneous changes in the political system (political decentralization, proportionality in parliament, decision-making), in policies (target groups, level of intervention, priorities of policy fields), and in management itself (in general or in finance in particular) the attribution of effects is not easy. Societal effects may be due to politics and/or policy and/or public management.

However, this does not mean that a relatively acceptable convergence of visions of trajectories is possible, based on some inner knowledge of the countries under scrutiny.

2. THE FINANCIAL MANAGEMENT TRAJECTORY

Here, the modernization of the practice of financial management is linked to a theoretical framework. A first section deals with the broader context of budgeting, financial management and the link with performance in government, and focuses particularly on the innovation of performance budgeting in a framework of performance management. The second section is about models explaining modernization. The next sections discuss budgeting, accounting and auditing. Finally, the matter of a driving force is discussed.

2.1 Budgeting, Financial Management and Performance

For a long time, budgeting appeared to be quite a separate field of administrative reality. This resulted in segregated and new theories or constructs of ideas and also in distinct theories in existing social sciences (Rubin, 1988). Its major concern was to theoretically describe an empirical process of allocating limited financial resources in a context of policy and politics (Schick, 1988). Economics (e.g., cost-benefit analysis, taxing policies, economic implications of budgetary policies); political sciences (e.g., lobbying, incrementalism, history of institutions); and public administration and public management (e.g., zero-based budgeting, management by objectives, planning programming budgeting system) all looked at this budgetary process from different angles.

The financial management cycle (budgeting, accounting and auditing) is one important expression of a broader policy cycle (preparation, decision, implementation and evaluation). It is not surprising that ministries of finance, budget control departments, and inspections of finance, auditor generals and the like develop dominating strategies of modernization. Financial cycles (budget, accounts and audits) are recurrent and their procedures are unavoidable and enforceable.

The choice for a specific way in which policy makers and managers guide, control and evaluate their organization should determine an organization's choice for a financial system.

Three key questions in organizations are answered by three major components in a financial system (Table 2.1).

Table 2.1
Questions for Financial Systems

Budget and Guidance	Accounts and Control	Audit and Evaluation
What can we do? What shall we do in the next period?	What is happening during the implementation?	What did we do? How did we do this in the past period?

Ideally, a good financial system develops and connects the practice of budget, accounts and audits, and takes the cost of information into account.

For purposes of guidance, budgets should answer questions about what is possible with the budgetary coffers, and what shall be done in the next period. For purposes of control, accounting systems help tell what is happening, e.g., in the field of cost and expenses. For purposes of evaluation (value for money), audits should provide information about what happened and to what extent this happened in an economic, efficient and effective way, assuming a normal financial and compliance audit.

Performance budgeting and performance management become a common denominator in many improvement strategies.

Ideally, there are several possible scopes for budget systems with varying formats and criteria for change of budgetary volumes and allocations, as depicted in Table 2.2.

Some historical and present examples are the traditional line-item budgets which are input focused and formatted and almost always incrementally based (1A). It is possible to think of a line-item budget which is fully zero-based (1C). However, this is not very common. In periods of substantial savings a line-item focus may be combined with a partial zero-based change pattern (1B). The same applies to other examples which could easily be in a different box of Table 2.2, e.g., a performance-oriented budget could be subject to an incremental change (3A) or to a fully zero-based consideration (3C).

Table 2.2
Focus of Budget and Focus of Change

Focus of Change	Format of Budget			
	1. Input Format	2. Activities Format	3. Output Format	4. Effect Format
A. Incremental change	1A. Traditional line-item budget	2A	3A	4A
B. Partial zero-based change	1B	2B. Activity-based budgets	3B. Performance-oriented budget	4B
C. Full zero-based change	1C	2C	3C	4C. Planning programming budgeting system

The choice for a particular budget system is important since it determines the capacity to question the policy and management cycle further on. A line-item budget is too limited to develop, e.g., value for money audits, which requires at least an output-focused and effect-oriented budget system. The juxtaposition of two examples, as provided in Table 2.3, should demonstrate this.

International practice shows developing and evolving financial information systems with different degrees of success. Most countries are progressing with trial and error.

To analyse these evolutions scientifically, at least three steps should be taken:

1) Describe what changes are taking place, where, when, how and for what reason. OECD surveys provide significant information in this field (OECD, 1995). Also single country case studies are valuable (e.g., Lüder, 1994);

2) Explain these changes and their features, using theoretical frameworks or theories;

3) Predict changes and develop variables that will determine success or failure. Here, the study of the learning cycles is important. Yet, different administrative and political cultures do not always allow for a transfer, even an adapted one, of strategies, tactics, tools and techniques.

Table 2.3

Input- and Output-Oriented Financial Management Systems:
Comparing Positions 1A and 3B (Questions and Answers)

	Input-Formatted Budget (Line-Item)	Output-Formatted Budget (Performance-Oriented Budget)
Budget format: Q: What can we do? What shall we do in the next period?	A: This amount of money will be spent on personnel, subsidies, etc.	A: This amount of money will be spent to provide these services for these purposes.
Budget change: Q: How are budgets evolving?	A: Mostly in an incremental way	A: Mostly in a partially zero-based way
Accounts: Q: What is happening during implementation?	A: The money is being spent in such a way	A: Costs, service volumes and quality are evolving in such a way
Audits: Q: What did we do? How did we do this in the past?	A: This amount of money has been spent, according to rules and regulations	A: This amount of money has been spent, according to rules and regulations. This also happened with these degrees of economy, efficiency and effectiveness
Link between budget, accounts and audits	Disconnected in time	More connected in a management and policy cycle

2.2 Explaining Modernization of Financial Management

Literature on the basic technical elements of financial management, budgeting, accounting and auditing is widely available, (e.g., Rabin, 1992; Harper, 1989; Chambers ea. 1987). Theories on budgeting (e.g., Rubin, 1988), accounting and auditing are also available, be it to a lesser extent. There is also discussion on the degree of normativeness of these "empirical" theories and the validity of hidden assumptions. (In public administration and management: performance budgeting is better than another budgeting system; in political science: incrementalism is better than zero-based techniques; in economics: higher efficiency is better than lower efficiency.)

Literature explaining empirically why specific types of budgeting, accounting and auditing appear in specific places and at specific times, or predicting the development of new types and their degree of sustainability, is rare.

Lüder's model explaining and predicting governmental accounting innovations is based on the paradigm of contingency (Lüder, 1994). His modified contingency model of public sector accounting innovations explains the results of a financial management innovation process.

The relevant independent variables are (Lüder, 1994:9):

- societal structural variables (i.e., societal structure, capital market, organized pressure groups);
- political structural variables (i.e., political culture, political system and political competition);
- administrative structural variables (i.e., administrative culture, staff formation system, standard-setting organization, organizational characteristics regarding accounting);
- environmental stimuli (i.e., fiscal stress, financial scandals, dominating doctrine, change of parliamentary majority).

These variables affect the expectations and the behaviour of the general public, political actors and the administrative actors.

If implementation barriers (e.g., the legal system, size of jurisdiction, staff qualifications) are surmounted, a renewed and modernized financial management may occur.

The whole discussion about causality, and sufficient and necessary reasons, is theoretically complex and empirically difficult to check, since the research methods do not allow for experimental or quasi-experimental designs. Only multi-case studies are possible and acceptable.

A systems-analysis-developed checklist of determining variables is useful. Yet, it is tempting to use this as a mechanical way to explain and then to predict changes, or to develop variables determining success and failure.

It is interesting to read that Buschor draws a causal picture going from advanced public accounting via performance measurement to new public management (Buschor, 1994). This means that there is a pattern of change and evolution from a technical tool to an activity and process, and further on to a broader practice, culture and paradigm. Here, too, it is tempting to take a causal mechanistic and behaviourist stand.

The whole question of sustainable modernization should be disentangled as follows:

- what is the origin of an innovation? (creation and (deutero)-learning);
- how should one turn an innovation into a routine? (implementation and (double-loop) learning);
- how should one keep the new routine running? (incentives and (single-loop) learning);
- how should one spread the innovation and new routine? (expansion and all types of learning).

It is intriguing to see that Anglo-American and Scandinavian academics and practitioners are taking the lead in public management innovations. It is interesting to see that these changes are (blindly) considered to be improvements, although few have been evaluated critically. It is remarkable that, e.g., Latin and "Rechtsstaat" oriented countries apparently are wrestling more with these concepts and practices than others.

Finally, it is paradoxical that economic giants, e.g., in Germany and Japan, are almost absent on the list of "public sector innovators." It suffices to consult the OECD management surveys (OECD, 1995) to see their contrasting positions.

Yet, Germany has its own and adapted quality improvement strategy and strategies for public sector modernization (Pollitt and Bouckaert, 1995; Klages and Haubner, 1995). Excellent private sector economic performance seems not to coincide necessarily with a public sector administrative performance that is high on the agenda. Unless the German public performance is of a sufficient high level there is no need to change priorities. But, others who look at themselves as having serious public management problems do not consult, let alone copy, the good German Weberian bureaucracy and its valuable model of the Rechtsstaat. To the contrary, the UK is moving into another direction: the market state.

Variables that do make a significant difference are, among other elements:

- the budgetary crisis and the related ascension of economic rationalism (e.g., Australia and New Zealand);
- the existence and tradition of decentralization that creates more degrees of freedom, smaller bureaucracies and a closer monitoring of stakeholders (e.g., in Scandinavian countries);
- the absence of a rigid, well-developed and comprehensive administrative legislation creating results-oriented frameworks rather than procedure- and activity-determined prescriptions (e.g., in the UK).

A final question is how sustainable these modernization initiatives will be, and whether it is possible to predict the degree of sustainability? In Canada, the valuable Improved Ministerial Authority and Accountability (IMAA) that provided information on performance for guidance, control and accountability collapsed under its own bureaucratic weight. Crucial variables are institutional tradition and culture and political and administrative initiative and momentum.

A key element in performance management modernization is the development of an adjusted and modernized financial set of tools. Key elements are the development of new systems of budgeting, of accounting, of auditing and of links between these three pillars.

The trajectories inside the components are quite similar.

2.3 The Budget Trajectory

Budgets are all tending towards covering more functions at the same time. Two important functions are the macro-economic focus and the managerial focus which are significantly emphasized in budget reforms.

According to Caiden (1988: 48) the non-market allocation of financial resources shifted from pre-budgeting to budgeting and now to a super-budgeting status. This means that super-budgets are conceived as systems interacting with other systems, not processes. Others call this macrobudgeting (LeLoup, 1988) or meta-budgeting. This coincides well with changes in the functions of budgeting, and the related management agenda (Bouckaert and Van Reeth, 1998). Budgeting is going beyond a mere process of resource allocation. It is a system which is focusing simultaneously on planning, allocation of resources, flexibility, economic guidance, integration of individual budget decisions and evaluation, and control of proliferated activities (Caiden, 1988). Budgeting is also increasingly interacting with internal systems. Budgeting starts including implementation and evaluation which are major elements in a broader managerial system, not just a separate process in a political context. This is the reason why guidance of the budget system is subject to modernization due to changes in management, control and accountability.

The macro-economic focus required a reduction of the level of expenses that is measured in terms of budget deficits and the budget share of the GDP. This resulted in two savings strategies using different trajectories of macrobudgeting.

A first trajectory was a rather linear and top-down cut back in which budget ceilings were set at the political level. This was the case in Canada and the Netherlands. In the Netherlands this was called the *cheese-slice* method. The number of rounds and the speed of slicing resources depended on the budgetary necessity and the political opportunities to do so. This purely input-oriented focus disturbed the parallel trajectory of performance orientation to the extent that the two were detached and that the available resources became unpredictable over the coming years. This resulted in a partial opposition of the macro-economic function and the management function of budgeting and the budget cycle. This also resulted in a stronger role of the budget department compared to the management departments in the ministry of finance (or the Treasure Board Secretariat).

A second trajectory was to shift to *frame budgeting* as, e.g., in Sweden and Finland. This was an amendment to the traditional bottom-up approach in guiding this with a budget frame. This resulted in redesigning the budget cycle in a two-stage cycle. First, there is a political discussion on the funds for each ministry with feedback information on results. Second, there is a discussion between ministries and agencies on the contracts and the performance to be delivered. This guided bottom-up approach probably resulted in a better match of the macro-economic agenda and the managerial performance agenda. Also, the potential polarization between the budget department and the management department was less explicit. Finally, the time scale for stability of the budget, at least in Sweden, was originally set at three years, then at six years. Ultimately this seemed impossible to maintain because of the tremendous budgetary pressure itself.

Finland also added an innovation by allowing *net budgeting*. This means that a net amount is in the budget and that additional resources could (partly) be kept in the agency itself, e.g., in the Patent Agency. This marries the macro-economic and the managerial concerns rather well.

The managerial focus in the budgetary process implies that budgets become more performance oriented. The degree of performance-orientedness and the format of budget documents differ. One could distinguish between three positions that may accumulate and create different trajectories.

First, some budgets started including some performance indicators as illustrations of the activities and outputs delivered. A second position is not only to add performance indicators but to change the format of the document and to enrich the content in relating other documents to the budget discussion, e.g., Annual Reports (Sweden and Finland) or Business Plans (internal and confidential) and Reports on Plans and Priorities (Canada). A third position is to add a change of procedure and timing in order to influence the debate and the decision-making of the allocations in the interaction of ministries with agencies, inside government and between government and parliament.

Table 2.4

Trajectories of Budget Systems

Budget Status		Countries
Input-oriented line-item budget		Initial positions: France, Germany, Netherlands, Canada, Sweden, Finland, Australia, New Zealand, USA, UK, EU.
A:	include some performance information	I: EU
A+B:	change format and content and add other documents	II: Netherlands, USA
A+B+C:	adapt procedures and timing	III: Canada, Sweden, Finland, UK, Australia, New Zealand

In Canada, the combination of the Policy and Expenditure Management System (PEMS), the Multi-Year Operational Plan (MYOP) and the Operational Framework Plan (OFP) in 1981 was a major shift toward a comprehensive vision which affected the content, with indicators, the format and the context of other supporting documents and the timing and procedure. The level of analysis was on programs and activities. This was amended with Improved Ministerial Authority and Accountability (IMAA) in 1986 and with Memoranda of Understanding (MOU) in 1988. However, this became burdened with red tape and was diluted in practice. The 1994 reforms resulted in the Ex-penditure Management System (EMS) with Business Plans and Reports on Plans and Priorities, with performance architecture Planning Reporting and Accountability Structure (PRAS) with business lines at the level of organization that may be consolidated.

In Sweden the results based management of 1988 resulted in depth budget requests and a "reglerinsbrev." This was amended and changed in 1993 in New Budgeting and Accounting Forms with a two-stage budget request, *reglerinsbrevs* and Annual Reports in a new time frame. A similar change happened in Finland with the 1989 State Budget Reform with a performance orientation in 1990. This was amended in the 1993 Management by Results initiative with the two-stage budget request procedure, the contracts and the annual reports in an adapted time frame.

In the Netherlands, the Financial Accountability Operation from 1986 till 1992, the requirement included policy evaluation programmes in the budget (1992) and the step-wise increase of performance information (estimates in 1990, outputs in 1997, efficiency in 1998 and scheduled effects in 1999) demonstrate that there is a different trajectory. Also, in the USA, the Governmental Performance Results Act (GPRA) resulted in an obligation for budgetary documents to include performance-related information.

The European Union shifted to the "Fiche Financière" which had to include some information on performance. However, this was a difficult and *ad hoc* operation which is part of the Sound and Efficient Management 2000 (EU Commission) and seems to be barely evolving at all. France and Germany seem not to be engaged in a trajectory of performance-oriented budget changes (Pain, 1998).

Finally the shift toward accrual budgeting is perceived by some as feasible and in an experimental stage. This applies mostly to the operational budget of entities.

2.4 The Accounting Trajectory

Accounting systems are all tending toward a shift from cash-based accounts to general double-bookkeeping with balance sheets and results-and-cost accounts. Accrual accounting seems also to be a major shift in many organizations.

Three positions could be distinguished. First, there is the traditional cash-based cameralistic accounting system. Second, there is a shift to double-bookkeeping, with possibly some elements of cost calculation. Third, there is an extended and comprehensive accrual accounting system with cost analysis and supported by a performance measurement system.

There are different trajectories that are observed. A first trajectory is to remain in the cash-based system which means a minor movement without progress. In the Netherlands the government decided (2000) not to have the cash-based accounting system for the ministries. This also implies that the links between expenses and costs or between costs and performance become difficult to demonstrate. Also in Canada, the PRAS and the Business Plans based on business lines suggest an enriched cameralistic system. However, at this stage the Treasury Board Secretariat (TBS) and the General Accounting Office (GAO) are studying the implementation of double-bookkeeping which is absent for the moment.

Table 2.5
Accounting Trajectories

Accounting Status	Country
A: cash-based system	Initial position: Netherlands, Finland, Sweden, Canada, Denmark, Australia, New Zealand, USA, France, Germany, EU.
B: double-bookkeeping	II: USA, Netherlands, Finland
C: accrual accounting with extended cost calculation supported by performance measurement system	III: Sweden, New Zealand, Australia, UK

A second trajectory is the shift to double-bookkeeping. Finland made an effort to move to double-bookkeeping in 1992. However, this project remained in the pilot project stage. In 1998 the decision was taken again to shift to double-bookkeeping. In the Netherlands, the government also decided that agencies should have double-bookkeeping. Reality shows that not all agencies respond to this requirement.

A third trajectory is to move to an extended system of accrual accounting with cost calculation and supported by Performance Measurement System (PMS). In Sweden there is a well developed performance accounting system with an external and an internal accounting system. The external system is for purposes of accountability, the internal system, based on a data warehouse of object codes (organization, product, activity, etc.) is for managerial purposes. This is also the case in Australia and New Zealand where capital costs are included in cost accounting systems.

In France, Germany and the European Union, a cash-based accounting system seems to be the present state of the art.

In conclusion, the major differences are in the degree of detail of cost-accounting systems, the link with performance measurement systems and the extent of application which means that agencies are sooner involved than ministries in modernized accounting systems.

2.5 The Audit System

Audit systems are all tending toward going beyond the traditional financial and compliance auditing (A). A second, intermediate position is to enrich the traditional audit with some *ad hoc* studies on performance of an organization or evaluation of a programme (B). A third position is a fully developed and institutionalized performance audit in the system (C). This last position includes an analysis of economy, efficiency and effectiveness.

Table 2.6
Audit Trajectories

Audit Status	Country
A: traditional financial and compliance audit	Initial position: Netherlands, Sweden, Finland, Canada, Denmark, Australia, New Zealand, USA, France, Germany, EU.
B: traditional audit enriched with some elements of performance and evaluation	I: France, EU, Germany
C: institutionalized financial, compliance and performance auditing	II: Netherlands, Sweden, Finland, Canada, UK, USA, Australia, New Zealand

A first trajectory implies that performance auditing is institutionalized with a developed organizational unit, qualified personnel and a working schedule. This is the case in the Netherlands, Sweden, Finland, Canada, the USA, Australia and New Zealand. The large amount of countries in this cluster or trajectory differs significantly in at least four areas.

First, the institutional weight of performance audits differs. In some countries, e.g., Finland, the amount of public enterprises allocated to performance-related audits exceeds the numbers for traditional audit tasks. In many other countries this is not the case.

Second, the content of the performance-related audits differs. These audits could include a critical evaluation of the data sources; a verification of the numerically calculated data; an evaluation on the applicability and desirability of the methods used; an evaluation of the missing components in an analysis; and an evaluation of the conclusions of the analysis. And even within one of these tasks, there are major differences. The audit of performance data, e.g., is not evenly executed in the different countries under scrutiny. In Finland the financial auditors look at performance-related information. In other countries, like the Netherlands, this practice is in development. Also, in the USA, the General Accounting Office (GAO) develops substantial audits, whereas in Sweden, the National Audit Office (RRV) focuses on the audit of audits.

Third, the link between internal and external audit is different. For an external audit institution it is crucial to have an internal vector from which it can start working. In Canada, all departments have internal audit services and evaluation services, which may or may not coincide. All Dutch departments have audit services which are focused on the accounts but increasingly include performance related tasks. In Finland, internal audit is being organized but is not generalized. In Sweden, a 1995 government decision requires that some agencies have an internal audit service. The different degrees of internal audit will influence the quality and the role of the external audit services.

Fourth, the relationship of audit and evaluation varies. In the Netherlands, recurrent evaluation of policies has been separate from audits. In Canada, the evaluation of programs was a distinct effort in a savings context and was concentrated in time.

A second trajectory implies a shift where some elements of performance orientation are added to the traditional audit. This is not institutionalized but *ad hoc* in terms of organizational setting, personnel and choice of projects. France, some German Länder (not the federal level) and the European Court of Audit seem to correspond to this situation. However, the traditional financial and compliance audit is still extremely dominant and the performance parts are exceptional.

2.6 Generators of Change

Next to the choice of trajectories for budgets, for accounts and for audits, which are ultimately accumulating stages in similar directions, there is a major difference in combining these trajectories. The question of what is or should be the generating component of financial modernization—budget, accounting system or audit—is not resolved (or resolvable). Practice shows that different countries follow different patterns and trajectories in combining the components of the financial function.

A first trajectory follows the logical chain of financial events. Budgets are the first to modernize, then accounts should follow, and finally, audits. Since audits are part of an independent steering, the focus is more on the internal audit functions which follow the stream of information and the flux of documents. The initial Swedish case seems to confirm this trajectory. The Finnish case, all be it to a weaker and slower degree, seems also to confirm this pattern.

A second trajectory considers the accounting system as a pivot for the financial system. Budgets are derived from the accounts, as budgeted accounts. Audits are derived from accounts as audited accounts. No real examples seem available from this trajectory, except Sweden in a second stage of the first trajectory. In developing its performance accounting system, the budget and the audit were supported. To the extent that countries, like Australia, are expanding incremental budgeting, which is supposed to be based upon the (audited) accounting information, this also could be considered to be an accounting-based trajectory.

The third trajectory could suggest that audit is triggering change and pushing changes upstream. This is a fictitious and theoretical position in the public sector since budget systems, although voted by the legislator, are dominated by the executive. Accounting systems are developed in the executive. External audits are dependent on the legislative. The independence of the audit institutions results in another relationship rather than sequence or consequence. This could mean that changes in audit systems are not really connected to the changes in the budget system and the accounting systems. However, to the extent that internal and external audits are related, to the extent that parliament, through budget format discussions and audit reports, is active, this could be a relevant variable in steering changes in financial systems. Canada seems to have some features of this model, where the audit function was important in the momentum of change.

A fourth trajectory is a voluntary one where budget, accounts and audits are modernized (almost) simultaneously. This could also be said of New Zealand.

A fifth trajectory suggests a non-trajectory of disconnection between the three components. The Dutch example gives the impression of being disconnected. Budgets are enriched with evaluation materials (with performance-related indicators), and should have objectives. The critical reflections on the accounting system are totally detached from this, except perhaps in the discussion on their agencies. The audit office has taken an active part in pushing the executive to make objectives explicit. However, the strategy of the audit office seems rather divergent from the strategy of the ministry of finance. Table 2.7 provides an overview of the combined strategies and their (non-)coherence.

Table 2.7
Coherence of Some Trajectories
in Budgeting, Accounting and Auditing

Budget Status	Accounting Status	Audit Status	Coherence	Countries
Max	Max	Max	Strong	New Zealand, Australia
Max	Min/average	Max	Weaker	Finland, Canada
Max	Max	Min/average	Weaker	
Min/average	Max	Max	Weaker	
Min/average	Min/average	Max	Weak	Netherlands

Except for Sweden, New Zealand and Australia, none of the countries studied has a coherent strategy of modernizing the financial function.

3. LESSONS AND PRIORITIES FOR TRANSITION COUNTRIES

3.1 Consolidated Financial Trajectories
Could Be Facilitated by Having Common Objectives

There seem to develop three types of trajectories (ideal types) according to three main objectives of change: more savings (stability and resource allocation), better performance and enhanced accountability and control (Table 2.8 gives an example for some developed countries).

The combination of these three trajectories varies in intensity and this intensity varies over time. Also, it is sometimes difficult to allocate an initiative exclusively to one trajectory because of the interdependence of the other objectives.

Table 2.8
Conditions for Success: Global Trajectories

	Stability and Resource Allocation	Better Performance	Accountability
Canada	Program review Budget ceilings	Business plans PRAS (Planning Reporting and Accountability Structure) FIS (Financial Information Strategy) SOA (Special Operating Agencies) Performance audits	IRPP: Improved Reporting to Parliament PRAS: Government-wide Reporting
Sweden	Frame budgeting	In-depth budgets requests Internal accounting Performance audits Annual reports Results-based management	Annual reports VESTA: integrated, consolidated system for central government forecasting, budgeting, consolidated accounting, performance monitoring and payment information by 2000
Finland	Frame budgeting	Corporatization Management by results (Contracts)	Annual reports Governance project
The Netherlands	Key tasks and Reconsideration of tasks *Cheese-slice* method	Indicators in budget Evaluation review Interdepartmental audits Agencies Efficiency projects	Indicators in budget Interdepartmental audits

3.1.1 The Stability and Resource Allocation Trajectory

This trajectory focuses first and foremost on the reduction of deficits and the size of government: the higher the need to cut the spending, the lesser the degree of freedom to focus also on the performance improvement or accountability side. Performance is reduced to doing less and accountability is reduced to the input side.

All countries were initially subject to the savings trajectory. Some focused more on this and developed an input-oriented strategy; others combined it with some structural and procedural efforts focused on performance. As a result the input side of operations becomes the central focus, i.e., expense and cost. This also will imply a systematic and compulsory top-down approach with elements of cost-based market testing. Organizations will get reduced funds, personnel will be reduced without really asking how this will effect the outputs or the quality, financial incentives will be severely scrutinized and information systems will not prioritize output and effect indicators.

3.1.2   The Performance Trajectory

This trajectory focuses on improved internal functioning of the organization by using some external mechanisms (market testing, benchmarking, vouchers) and some internal mechanisms (performance-related budgets, accrual accounting, performance auditing, strategic planning, internal contract management, self-evaluations, etc.). This is clearly driven by a voluntary bottom-up approach. Incentive structures are developed and require information systems that are quite elaborate and sophisticated.

3.1.3   The Accountability Trajectory

The objective of improving the accountability process to higher levels of the executive, or to the legislative, or to the public requires a different set of instruments and another focus. Information systems will be crucial and the audit of these systems and their content will be indispensable for general debate and (contradictory) discussion. Contracts will be necessary to make resources and commitments explicit. Incentive systems will play an important part in giving accountability leverage. There is a need to structure this process; a top-down approach will be necessary to determine the rules of the game and to guarantee that all actors are involved.

It is obvious that some elements of these trajectories are not really and fully compatible. For example, top-down approaches, which seem more required for stability and accountability purposes should be combined with bottom-up approaches to improving performance itself.

3.2 A Common Conceptual and Procedural Framework Would Support a Sustainable Financial Management

In the field of financial management there is a need for a generally accepted framework focusing on effectiveness, efficiency, economy and quality.

Figure 2.1
Policy Cycle—Conceptual Framework

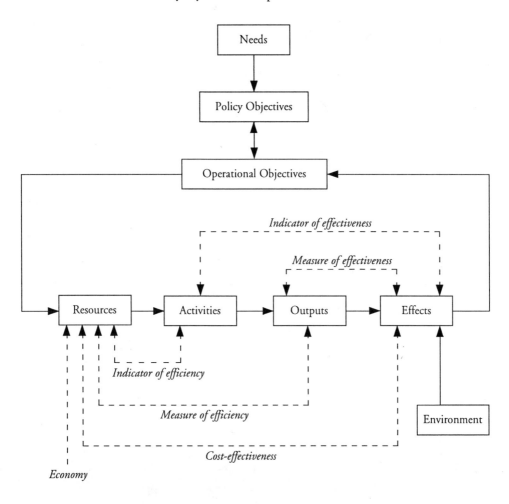

This conceptual and procedural framework is developed in Figures 2.1 and 2.2. The conceptual framework, as described in Figure 2.1, is a cycle of operational objectives, which redefine general policy objectives representing societal needs, feeding into a chain of resources, activities, outputs and effects. These effects are influenced by environmental events and should match the (quantified) operational objectives. This conceptual framework should be used in a procedural cycle, as shown in Figure 2.2.

To be successful, it is necessary to develop and implement a conceptual, institutional and procedural cycle. This implies coherent procedures, converging visions, matching levels of informational and organizational transparency and corresponding and complementary institutional interests.

Figure 2.2
Procedural Cycle for Policy and Management

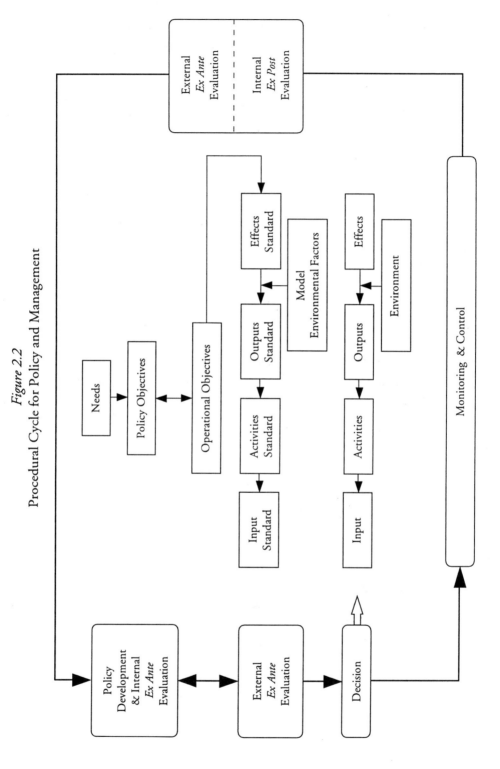

REFERENCES

Bouckaert, G.: "Remodelling Quality and Quantity in a Management Context" in Halachmi, A. and Geert Bouckaert, (eds.): *Public Productivity through Quality and Strategic Management*, (Amsterdam: IOS, 1995), pp.21–38.

Buschor, E.: "Introduction: From Advanced Public Accounting via Performance Measurement to New Public Management" in Buschor, E. and K. Schedler, (eds.): *Perspectives on Performance Measurement and Public Sector Accounting*, (Bern: Haupt, 1994), pp.vii–xviii.

Caiden, N.: "Shaping Things to Come" in Rubin, I. (ed.): *New Directions in Budget Theory*, (Albany: SUNY-Press, 1988), pp.43–58.

Chambers, A., G. Selim and G. Vinten: *Internal Auditing*, (Pitman: London, 1987).

Harper, W. M.: *Management Accounting*, (London: Pitman, 1989).

Klages, H. and O. Haubner: "Strategies for Public Sector Modernization" in Halachmi, A. and Geert Bouckaert, (eds.): *The Enduring Challenges in Public Management*, (San Fransisco: Jossey Bass, 1995), pp.348–376.

Lüder, K. "The 'Contingency Model' Reconsidered" in Buschor, E. and K. Schedler, (eds.): *Perspectives on Performance Measurement and Public Sector Accounting*, (Bern: Haupt, 1994), pp.1–15.

OECD: *Management Survey*, 1995, (Paris: OECD, 1995).

Pollitt, Christopher and Geert Bouckaert: *Public Management Reform*, (Oxford: Oxford University Press, 2000).

Pollitt, Christopher and Geert Bouckaert, (eds.): *Quality Improvement in European Public Services*, (London: Sage, 1995).

Rabin, J. (ed.): *Handbook of Public Budgeting*, (New York: Marcel Dekker, 1992).

Rubin, I. (ed.): *New Directions in Budget Theory*, (Albany: SUNY-Press, 1988).

CHAPTER 3

Local Government Budgeting: The CEE Experience

Mihály Hőgye

■

Charles McFerren

Table of Contents

1. Introduction 47

2. Environment: The Local Government System 48
    2.1 Procedural and Management Issues 48
    2.2 Legal Control and Audit 49
    2.3 Structure of Local Budgets 50
    2.4 Information Systems 51

3. Process: Local Government Budgeting 51
    3.1 Timing and Time Scale 51
    3.2 Decision-Making Process 54
    3.3 Implementation 56
    3.4 Internal Reallocation of Appropriations 58
    3.5 Off-Budget Funds 58
    3.6 Budgeting Techniques 60
    3.7 Audit Process: External and Internal 62

4. Conclusion and Recommendations 64
    4.1 Decentralization 65
    4.2 Expenditures 66
    4.3 Funding Predictability 66
    4.4 Capital Expenditures 67
    4.5 Budgeting Process 67
    4.6 Human Resources 68
    4.7 Planning 68
    4.8 Asset Management 69
    4.9 Transparency and Publicity 69

Notes 70

List of Tables and Figures

Table 3.1: Cash Management 57

Figure 3.1: Institutional Control Structures 50
Figure 3.2: Timing Issues 52
Figure 3.3: Participants in the Decision-Making Process 55
Figure 3.4: The Local Government Budget Is Just the Tip of the Iceberg.............. 59
Figure 3.5: A Model for Best Practice Transfer 64

Local Government Budgeting: The CEE Experience

Mihály Hőgye and Charles McFerren

1. INTRODUCTION

Although public finance comprises a significant, if not dominant, part of all developed economies and thus directly affects the lives of all its citizens, the existing analytical framework is still significantly underdeveloped compared to that of corporate finance. Whereas Fisher significantly simplifies the analysis of corporate finance problems with the proof of his Separation Theorem showing the importance of efficient capital markets, which explicitly guides managers to concentrate on the maximization of wealth without considering the wants of stockholders, no similar theoretical guidelines exist for public servants genuinely striving to satisfy the wants of their constituents.[1] While Arrow has provided a general framework for the analysis of choice in the public framework, it remains too abstract for practitioners faced with the day-to-day task of Public Expenditures Management (PEM).[2] Within the field of public finance, material concerning local government budgeting is lacking. Thus, the current state-of-the-art provides little theoretical guidance for local government employees charged with satisfying the wants of their constituents.

As in the natural sciences, theory in the social sciences is very much dependent on reliable data—the absence of which makes it impossible to separate good from bad theory. The purpose of this work is to fill an existing void in descriptive data concerning local government budgeting in Central and Eastern European countries (CEE). In the terms of reference given to the project teams chosen for each of the countries included in the study, the project was designed to elicit three types of information: (1) the budgeting environment, (2) the budget process and (3) a summary of best practices.

Any prescriptive theory of local government budgeting in CEE countries must explicitly take into account the legal structure and the government institutions that make up the budgeting environment within which a manager must operate. But this is not sufficient to model the actions of managers. In the decision-making process, managers are also strongly affected by their internal value systems with regard to questions of "best" or "desirable." Finally, to complete the descriptive model of a local government budgeting system, a description of the budgeting process from the start through the execution to the final audit is necessary. For the country-specific details concerning these three types of information, the reader is guided to the following country studies in Part II. What follows is a summary of the important results of the country studies along with recommendations for future research.

2. ENVIRONMENT: THE LOCAL GOVERNMENT SYSTEM

As in the private sector, all managers working in local government must adapt to their environment. To properly understand the budgeting system existing in a country, it is necessary to understand the legal framework guiding and limiting managerial actions as well as the various governmental organizations with which managers must interact. An analysis of the country studies highlights the following important factors affecting management decisions.

2.1 Procedural and Management Issues

Although important in all developed countries, the following aspects of local government in CEE countries are of particular importance: (1) the dependence on ministries, (2) the varying degrees of influence of national local government associations and (3) internal political conflicts.

One measure of the degree of decentralization of government in a country is the autonomy of local government from the various governmental agencies. As would be expected, a broad range of possibilities are represented in the countries included in this study. The extreme position is represented by Albania, where the government ministries control such vital functions as the distribution of budgeted funds, the capital expenditure decisions by project, financial and staffing decisions for the public utility companies and the management and privatization of all assets. At this extreme, local government has responsibilities, but very little real authority.

In all countries represented in the study, one or more local government associations existed for the purpose of representing local government interests at the national level. These associations range from the informal to formal, with the associated degrees of effectiveness. Bulgaria provides a good example of such effective associations. In Bulgaria, there are special fields within which target bodies are established. They are not part of the municipal system, but the participation of municipalities is necessary and most important. For example, to promote the policy on economic social cohesion and regional development, by a decree of the Council of Ministers, a Commission on Economic and

Social Cohesion was formed to coordinate and facilitate the interactions of municipalities, the national government and international agencies. Obviously, the effectiveness of such an association with strong central support is greater than the informal and underdeveloped structure existing in many of the countries.

Finally, it must be remembered that a budget is the result of a political process. Both efficiency and effectiveness are enhanced if competing political parties can be motivated to work together. An example of an unusual method to achieve this goal congruence is found in Hungary. There, in many municipalities, the city mayor is responsible for submitting the budget proposal to the municipal body. In one example given in the country study, the budgeting process is smoothed by the involvement of six consultants (each representing a particular field, e.g., civil service, tax policy, economy, etc.) with various political party affiliations that jointly work out the budget proposal with the mayor. In this way, most political disagreements are eliminated before the budget proposal is even submitted.

2.2 Legal Control and Audit

The central government always maintains some control over the municipalities. For analysis purposes, this control can be examined in two dimensions: (1) the target of the control and (2) the institutional form. The target of the control concerns what is being audited and is described in detail in section 3.

With respect to the institutional forms of control, two basic structures emerge from the country analysis. In the Agency system, many field offices monitor the operations of the lower levels of government. Each ministry involved in local affairs has its own agency. Because each of these agencies have equal authority and only exercise an oversight function, the effect of this system is to decentralize authority to lower levels of government. In the Prefect system, effective central control is maintained with the use of a State Administration with field offices at the local level. In addition to exercising an oversight function, these offices have significant responsibilities (e.g., authorizing cash disbursements) during the budget preparation and implementation stages. These two structures are compared in Figure 3.1.

Hungary and Bulgaria provide good examples of the two structures. The Hungarian system is a typical Agency system. Almost every ministry has field offices, but the most important is the County Public Administration Office, which is the agency of the Prime Minister's Office. This office has the responsibility for investigating the legality and regularity of local decisions. If decisions on minor issues do not conform with the law, this agency can overturn them. In all other cases involving municipal decrees, the agency's only course of action is to request a change from the municipality—a change cannot be imposed from above.

49

Figure 3.1
Institutional Control Structures

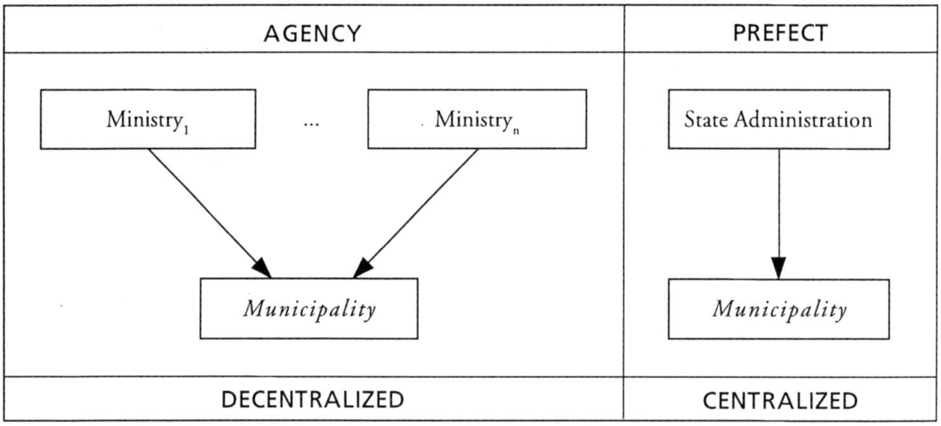

AGENCY		PREFECT
Ministry₁ ... Ministryₙ		State Administration
Municipality		Municipality
DECENTRALIZED		CENTRALIZED

In Bulgaria, the National Budget Procedures Act requires that the Audit Office *exercise control over the implementation* of the national budget in accordance with the Audit Office Act. Internal government financial control is organized by the Ministry of Finance through the Agency for State Internal Financial Control and exercises control over the financial activities of municipalities. This internal government financial control extends to the financial activities of:

1. The beneficiaries of central government loans as well as those of the European Union program funds;
2. The local tax authorities responsible for collecting revenues for the central budget;
3. The beneficiaries of the off-budget accounts and the funds under the State Budget Act of the Republic of Bulgaria;
4. The beneficiaries of budget funds contained in municipal budgets;
5. The activities of entities financed from the central government budget, the municipal budget or the programs of the European Union.

Thus, a significant element of central control remains during the implementation of the municipal budget.

2.3 Structure of Local Budgets

In general, to facilitate consolidation and inter-regional comparisons, the central government provides a standard chart of accounts that all budgeting units must adhere to. In Croatia, however, the Ministry of Finance does not prescribe the classification of the budget by cost type or by function. Instead, expenditures are classified only according to administrative categories (i.e., budgetary beneficiaries and purposes) and no classification of expenditures in terms of programs, sub-programs or categories of activities is provided. Obviously, this system makes any but the most rudimentary analysis of the budget impossible.

Similarly, most countries at least make an attempt to separate capital and operating expenditures. However, this is not always the case. In Estonia, for example, the municipal budget is not formally required to have separate budgets for operating expenses and for capital budgeting. The justification given for this by the Ministry of Finance is that international standards established by the IMF do not imply the use of a separate capital budget. Although not required by a central authority, the larger cities are creating separate capital budgets, mainly due to the existence of large investment programs in which the lenders require that the use of all borrowed money be transparent.

2.4 Information Systems

As might be expected, information systems are a weak point in all countries, with Estonia representing a good example of the difficulties facing local governments. The reporting requirements to various institutions are extensive with many ministerial departments and government institutions requesting similar information. Rather than coordinating the information requirements and formats, the higher level authorities simply demand compliance from the local governments, thus imposing a large administrative burden. In addition, the frequent changes in format make it impossible to compare the reports from different years, so no detailed time-series analysis can be carried out. To make budgets a truly useful management tool, all reporting countries highlighted the necessity to significantly improve the existing information systems.

3. PROCESS: LOCAL GOVERNMENT BUDGETING

Many differences across countries in the process of local government budgeting are the direct result of the varying structural relationships existing among the different levels of government. Apart from these differences, the countries showed much variety in the following factors.

3.1 Timing and Time Scale

In order to be able to compare and contrast the budget process across countries, information was gathered concerning the timing of the various stages in the process and about the budgeting time horizon. Figure 3.2 summarizes the following timing issues identified by the respondents:

A. *Preparation:* When does the process begin and who is involved?

B. *Approval:* At what point does the budget become official so that implementation can begin?

C. *Publicity:* In what form is the budget disclosed to the wider public?

D. *Amendments:* What possibilities exist during the year to change the budget in any way?

E. *Closing:* When is the final report concerning the budget year issued?

F. *Capital Budgeting:* What modifications are made in the budget process to allow for projects extending beyond a single budget period?

Figure 3.2
Timing Issues

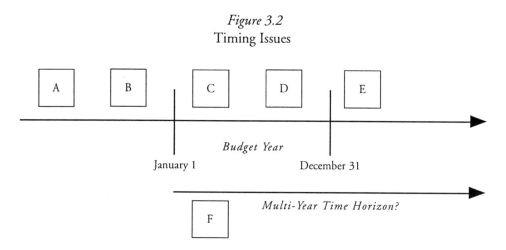

The budget process never really ends, with the planning for the next year's budget closely following the publication of the previous year's budget report. The *preparation* process formally begins with budget guidelines issued by central authorities six to nine months before the start of the budget year.[3] Thereafter, the process is continuous through the entire year and iterative with input coming both from above (e.g., estimates of grants and other transfers) and below (e.g., how funds should be spent).[4]

Theoretically, *approval* of the annual budget should be given before the start of the budget year so that the budget holders have clear guidelines. Practically, however, this is not possible because of the significant dependence on central transfers, which are only finalized as part of the State budget. Albania is representative of the normal procedure followed with small variations in all the countries:[5]

After the central budget is approved, the local government must "re-approve" its budget.... Local governing bodies approve the budget through a Local Council Decision. Once formally approved by the council, the financial office executes the budget.... If a local government's final conditional budget is not approved by December 31, which has occurred many times, the State budget provides monthly transfers for operations amounting to 1/12th of the previous year's funding. The independent budget must be approved by March 15 of the budget year.

For the countries in the study, formal approval of the budget is at the local government level, with a requirement to inform a central office of the final approved budget. Before formal approval, budget holders are allowed to make expenditures based on the previous year's budget.

Publicity is a weak point in the process in all of the countries. Typical of the responses was the following: "Information on the execution and closing of the municipal budget has to be made available to the public."[6] Nothing is said about the timing or the format, which probably means that some summary information of the final budget is distributed in a form probably incomprehensible to the layman. In none of the country studies did this receive much attention.

Amendments, on the other hand, were treated extensively. It seems that no country expected to get through the year without having to modify the budget. Hungary provides a good example of the rolling budget that each of the countries seems to employ:[7]

Most municipalities do not define explicitly the crisis situations requiring a modification in the local budget. Primarily, this is due to the fact that the local budget must be revised regularly every three months when the unplanned funds (e.g., from central transfers) must be recorded in the budget.

Thus, amendments are not only possible, they are planned for.

Where responding countries gave a date, the *closing* deadline was generally in mid-March of the following year.[8] As with the publicity requirement for the approved budget, the reporting requirements appears in all of the countries to be considered a mere formality. There appears to be no attempt in any of the countries to use the report to evaluate the performance of the budget holders against the agreed plan.

Since the cash-basis of accounting is the basis used in all the reporting countries, *capital budgeting* and the related issues of the asset register and depreciation schedules remains a real problem. With this issue, it is beneficial to read each of the country responses. The variety is due not so much because of substance (either they do or they do not), but more because of the wide range of justifications for *not using established capital budgeting techniques*. Hungary represents the most advanced stage before full implementation.[9] The legal framework exists; there is a central mandate to implement it and there is a general recognition that it is useful if not essential. The only problem is that lack of sufficient numbers of qualified personnel needed to implement the system. Estonia, on the other hand, where none of the structural requirements exist, gives an elegant justification for not implementing capital budgeting that is worth quoting in its entirety:[10]

> *The World Bank recommends the separation of capital and operating budget. But the Ministry of Finance (MoF) has decided to employ the international standards (Government Finance Statistics) established by the IMF—which does not imply the use of a separate capital budget. Therefore, the MoF has not established any requirements and methods to separate these two types of budgets. Presumably, in developed countries, this separation of budgets is a reasonable strategy. But in transition countries, the unification of the operating and capital budgets can have some advantages.*

Unfortunately, the list of possible advantages was not given. In summary, the issue of capital budgeting is interesting not because no country does it, but because of the varying degrees of understanding about its importance.

3.2 Decision-Making Process

The discussion of the decision-making process in local government budgeting is reminiscent of that distinguishing stockholder and stakeholder interests, but with an extension of the stakeholder idea on both sides. In government, as in the corporate world, budgets are used to allocate scarce resources to competing interests. What makes governmental budgeting more complex is the significant influence of the political process. Since governments exercise their allocative, stabilization and distributive functions[11] through budgets, they are political as well as economic documents and are products of the political processes by which competing interests in any nation achieve agreement.[12] Therefore, a description of the decision-making process involved in the local government budgeting necessarily depends on an understanding of the participants. As shown in Figure 3.3, the direct participants in the decision-making process are both strongly influenced by their constituents.

At the *local government level*, budget-making is primarily a policy process, possibly being the most important policy decision of the municipality. This process is a "multiple player game," in which every service department, institution, lobby and political party participate. The financial department and the head of the municipality (i.e., mayor) play the most important part in this process because they have to balance the competing demands of the line ministries and lobbies, while at the same time protecting the interests of the "whole population." The list of specific institutional names differs across reporting countries, but the principle is general—the final budget is the end result of a balancing act.[13]

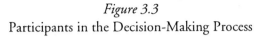

Figure 3.3
Participants in the Decision-Making Process

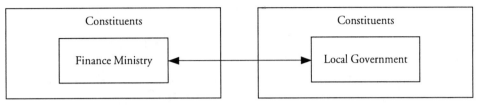

At the *central government level*, the Finance Ministry is ultimately responsible for all government budgeting. In addition to the problem of multiple constituents already discussed in relation to local government budgeting, there is the additional problem of conflicting laws emanating from the legislative body. Poland provides a good example of ambiguous legal environment within which the Finance Ministry must work.[14] There, the Law on Public Finances (central government) and the Law on Local Governments (municipalities) both explicitly give the following responsibilities to different institutions: guidelines concerning local government investment priorities, the privatization policy for the year, debt policy, as well as assumptions concerning such key parameters as inflation or expected economic growth. Thus, as was frequently reported by the countries, all participants must work within an ambiguous legal environment, which is expected to continue into the near future as the laws continue to evolve to give local governments more independence.

Finally, the *role of citizens* at both the central and local levels must be highlighted. In common with established democracies, the CEE countries included in this work also identified apathy and incomprehensibility of the budget as reasons for the non-participation of citizens in the process. But in addition to this, there is the element of newness such that the institutions and lawmakers are still struggling with the idea of what real role the average citizen should have. This is succinctly reported by Poland and is worth repeating here to summarize a general condition existing in all of the countries to a greater or lesser degree.[15]

> *The Polish regulatory regime does not require citizen participation in the budgetary process, though it does require that the budget be a public document and that council discussion of the budget be open to the public. At the same time, Polish law imposes no obstacles to increasing citizen participation in the budget process. Nonetheless, most Polish local government officials remain wary of public involvement and think that, in general, it causes more problems than it resolves. Moreover, local government officials have very little practical experience in this area. Finally, it has to be added that citizens generally think their public engagement ends at the ballot box and have, in general, shown little interest in the way that their elected officials spend public funds.*

3.3 Implementation

Concerning this research, the budget implementation concerns the question of cash management. The completed budget document is important as a road map, but it is also interesting to know who is driving the car. In conventional management literature, a distinction is made between responsibility (producing the budget, i.e., the road map) and authority (disbursing funds, i.e., the car driver). The research design explicitly took this distinction into account by separating budget production from cash management.

While acknowledging that there are many aspects of financial management, the scope of the research was limited to cash management, with the argument that it is the single best indicator of the degree of management autonomy at the local government level. As Horngren states:[16]

> *Decentralization is a matter of degree. Total decentralization means minimum constraints and maximum freedom for managers to make decisions at the lowest levels. Conversely, total centralization means maximum constraints and minimum freedom to make decisions.*

The research hypothesis was that countries can be differentiated by the degree of decentralization of the cash management of local governments.

Based on the responses of the countries in the study, two issues serve to separate the countries into the centralized and decentralized camps:
- Who worries about surpluses and deficits?
- Who signs the checks?

Taken together, the responses to these questions is sufficient to place the countries along a spectrum running from highly centralized to highly decentralized cash management. With these criteria, the results are summarized in Table 3.1.

Table 3.1
Cash Management

Centralized	Decentralized
Albania	Bulgaria
Croatia	Estonia
Poland	Hungary
Romania	
Russia	

NOTE: The order is alphabetical only and does not indicate a degree of intensity.

With respect to budget implementation, each of the countries should be reviewed separately due to the shades of their responses. For an example of *centralized cash management practices*, Russia is typical.[17] With respect to the question of *surpluses and deficits*, the process is highly centralized,

> *Institutions of the Central Bank of the Russian Federation and the authorized credit organizations make payments and calculations connected with the cash transfers of the budget. The basic operations concerning cash transfers of the budget are:*
> - *reception and transfer of funds collected as revenues of the budget;*
> - *sharing revenues from taxes and other revenues in the local budget;*
> - *distribution of budget funds within the limits of available funds on accounts.*

When funds are available, they are paid, subject to discretion of the central authority. When no funds are available, then negotiations start about raising funds, there being no clearly set funding responsibility at either the central or the local level. With respect to *authorizing cash disbursements*, the following is reported:[18]

> *To disburse cash from the local budgets, bodies of the Central Bank of the Russian Federation open the main operating account.*

The essence being that no funds are transferred until a central authority gives permission.

At the other extreme is Bulgaria, with perhaps the clearest statement of *decentralized cash management*:[19]

> *The Municipal Budgets Act identifies the legal independence of local governments in terms of authority to manage the cash flows: "the management of budgetary and extra-budgetary resources shall be carried out by the bodies of local government, the mayor and the municipal administration."*

Surpluses are not mentioned explicitly (probably because they are not a common occurrence), but *deficit* management is clearly the responsibility of local government:

> *Short-term borrowing is another important aspect of the municipal cash management. Legislation specifically allows municipalities to finance "deficits" up to 10% of own revenues.*

In summary, the working hypothesis was confirmed that the analysis of cash management practices is the key to understanding the degree of decentralization in the local government structure. That the topic is a sensitive one is evidenced by the intensity of the responses. Irregardless of the degree of decentralization already present, the local government responses unanimously recommended an extension.

3.4 Internal Reallocation of Appropriations

The ability to reallocate budgeted funds represents a source of political power at the local government level. To a greater or lesser extent, it is found in all the reporting countries, but is typically restricted with respect to amounts and with respect to the authorization process. Croatia represents the typical situation:[20]

> *The reallocation of the funds is allowed and possible among individual items of expenditure and individual budgetary beneficiaries. This reallocation is possible only with the approval of the head of the executive committee of the local government. If such approval is given, then the reallocation is implemented in such a way that the resources for a given item can be augmented by up to 5%, and the items for other beneficiaries or one other beneficiary can be diminished by the same amount.*

3.5 Off-Budget Funds

Budget systems commonly provide an option to form entities (e.g., foundations, companies, non-profit organizations) that are off-budget and manage off-budget funds. The budgeting issue with respect to these entities is one of transparency. Namely, when analyzing the existing and planned financial condition of local governments, is it possible to get a complete and accurate picture of all assets, liabilities and potential obligations? This is important for at least three reasons:

- *Country Credit Ratings.* Ultimately, the central authority is responsible for the financial conditions of local governments. Indeed, when assessing the creditworthiness of a country, international agencies such as the International Monetary Fund or the World Bank explicitly consider the total financial condition of the country at both the central and the local government levels.
- *Local Government Borrowing.* A goal expressed by each of the responding countries is the establishment of a bond market for local government issues. In order for a bond rating agency to be able to establish a rating of these issues, the total financial condition (including off-budget entities and related obligations) of the local government unit must be transparent.

- *Fraud.* Transparency is a significant fraud deterrent. Conversely, off-budget funds, coupled with the current weaknesses in the audit system, offer the potential for malfeasance.

The study was designed to elicit responses concerning: (1) consolidation practices for off-budget entities and (2) the use of guarantees from local governments to off-budget entities.[21] Figure 3.4 illustrates these issues.

Figure 3.4
The Local Government Budget Is Just the Tip of the Iceberg

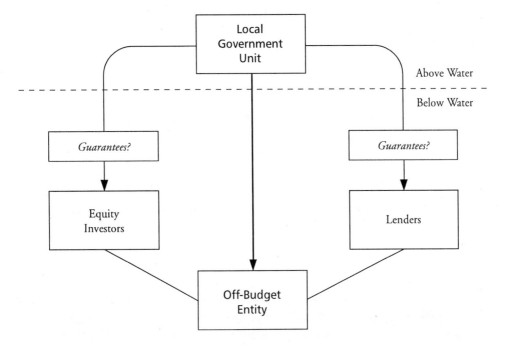

With this background, it is interesting to review the country responses. Given that the two issues of consolidation and of contingent liabilities (i.e., guarantees) are still very much debated in the corporate world, it is not surprising that no clear answers exist with regard to local government budgeting. Indeed, the respondents seem only to be tangentially aware of the issues (or not willing to discuss the individual country activities openly).

In general, *consolidation of off-budget entities* is not even an issue in the responding countries—it is simply not done. Either the respondents do not yet recognize this potential problem or, as in the case of Estonia, they are not yet affected by the consequences of not consolidating off-budget entities:[22]

> *The revenues from enterprises (dividends) may be included in the budget under the items "revenues from economic activities" or "dividends" or "other revenues." Many local governments do not have such items in their budgets because the companies do not operate at a profit.*

Despite the fact that off-budget entities are significant in all the reporting countries, this is the strongest statement recognizing that the local government should be the direct beneficiary. In all other countries, the existence is acknowledged, but the actual use is not analyzed in depth.

The issue of *guarantees* is even more problematic. In general, it appears that the potential consequences are not understood. In one of the few examples explicitly recognizing the existence of the problem, Croatia reports the following:[23]

> *Thus in the budgets of the local governments, there are transfers to the firms to finance losses and obligations, which they are unable to finance with their own resources. The position of the utilities is further complicated because they have the status of companies and are organized as joint stock companies, which turns their non-profit-making activity into a profit-making activity. Another problem is that the ownership of these companies is not clearly defined, nor are their rights and obligations with respect to the budgets of the local units.*

As could be expected, when negotiations take place between local government officials and entrepreneurs, a no-win situation occurs.[24] Albania shows this clearly as follows:[25]

> *In Tirana, there are about 50 enterprises that are "dependent" on the city. They are referred to as municipal enterprises, but no member from the municipality is included on the management board. They have a separate budget and their own account in the treasury system. For providing the service, the municipality allocates a part of its revenue to them.*

Thus, if the company is profitable, the private owners get the benefits. However, if it starts to lose money, then the local government must bail it out.

3.6 Budgeting Techniques

It is acknowledged that key differences in budgeting practices applied in the government and business sectors arise out of the differences in objectives: maximizing the collective satisfaction of the constituents versus maximizing the value of the entity. It is also acknowledged that significant developments have occurred in management control practices and procedures have been introduced in businesses worldwide in the recent past.[26] Despite the differences in objectives between government and business, it is interesting to evaluate the extent to which business current practices have affected local government budgeting practices. With this in mind, the research was designed to elicit responses about the following three issues:

- To what extent is *performance budgeting* (as opposed to line-item budgeting) used in practice?
- To what extent is *accrual accounting* used in addition to the mandatory *cash-based accounting*?
- To what extent is a *multi-year time horizon* used in the budgeting process?

From a long list of possibilities, these issues were chosen for analysis both because of their widespread acceptance and implementation (i.e., performance budgeting, accrual accounting and multi-year budgeting) in the corporate world, but also because of the seemingly obvious application in the local government environment. Thus the research question, "Is their application equally widespread in the CEE countries under review?"

Admittedly, the general response (i.e., no!) was somewhat expected, but again the shades of the responses was useful for evaluating the degree of development in the budgeting practices of the respondent countries. The following examples represents the cutting edge of budgeting practices in the subject countries.

In general, all the countries employed line-item budgeting techniques, which take into account only the previous year's cost of services or the costs related to operating the necessary institutions. However, there is a budding realization that the input (cost) is less significant than the output (performance). Thus, although not widespread, examples can be found of the use of different types of *performance budgeting systems*. Following Anthony and Govindarajan, performance budgeting systems can be classified based on what they purport to measure: (1) results measures, (2) process measures and (3) social indicators.[27]

A *results measure* (also known as outcomes measure) is a measure of output that is supposedly related to the organization's objectives. Bulgaria represents a frequently found example of this:[28]

> *A number of municipalities have developed performance indicators for some of the services under their full authority (waste disposal, street lighting) and implemented them into the budget process (e.g., tons of garbage collected, kilometers of roads resurfaced, number of drains maintained, cubic meters of water supplied).*

A *process measure* is related to an activity carried on by the organization. This is used, for example, in the program budgeting used in some cities in Hungary:[29]

> *These budgets contain detailed information about the "performance" of the different programs, but most of them measure only the "quantity" of the program (e.g., how many students attend any given school, how many meals are provided during the year in the public institutions, the size of the real estate used by the institution) and not the quality of the programs or the public satisfaction.*

A *social indicator* (e.g., the satisfaction of the citizens with local government services) is a broad measure of output that reflects the result of the work of the organization. Despite the measurement difficulties involved, social indicators can be useful for long-term evaluations of performance. Poland provides the only example of an attempt to measure social indicators:[30]

> *This evaluation is meant to address large issues such as what are our most important problems in each area and what are our most important goals. This sort of analysis is difficult because it requires gathering data not just on the unit costs of existing services, but also information on the quality of those services, citizens access to them, and perhaps most importantly whether citizens feel that these services are meeting their most important needs.*

The use of *accrual accounting* in addition to the mandatory cash-basis accounting is being discussed seriously in most of the countries, but there are no examples of an actual implementation. All respondents acknowledged the potential usefulness of the information provided by an accrual-based accounting system. However, until it becomes a legal requirement, it appears that in all of the reporting countries none of the scarce financial or human resources available to local governments will be used to implement such a system.

Similarly, the use of a *multi-year time horizon* in the budgeting process is agreed to be a good idea, but difficult to put into practice. Even in those countries where there is a legal requirement to use a multi-year time horizon, policy-makers give very little credence to the data in the budget document extending beyond one year.[31] The most commonly cited obstacle to extending the budgeting time horizon is accurate forecasting of future actions of the central government, since this represents the dominant source of funds for local governments.

3.7 Audit Process: External and Internal

The audit function provides the key feedback loop in the budgeting process. Without an effective audit, it is impossible to evaluate the efficiency and effectiveness of the budgeting system. To provide a framework for comparing the audit process in different countries, four elements must be described: (1) the auditor, (2) the authorization, (3) the subject of the audit and (4) the timing of the audit.

With respect to the auditor, responsibility for the audit function of municipalities can be found at three different levels: (1) within the municipality, (2) central audit office and (3) external private companies. While all countries reported a formal requirement for the establishment of an internal audit function at the municipal level, they typically followed Croatia's example of qualifying the requirement by stating that, despite the requirement, "…there is no organized internal control. The basic reason for this is the lack of qualified staff."[32] The primary audit control for all the countries remains very much centralized and vary only in degree. Albania's response is typical for very centralized structures when it writes, "The High State Control remains the highest institution controlling the entire activities of local government in Albania…."[33] The involvement of external auditing companies was frequently mentioned, but only with regard to publicly owned companies such as utilities or with respect to funds coming from international organizations such as the European Union.

Authorization is the formal acceptance of the local budget, thus giving the budget holders the right to make expenditures. One of the most important functions of the auditor is to make sure that all expenditures have been properly authorized. As might be expected, there was a wide range of responses regarding the level of authorization, ranging from complete centralization (e.g., Russia)[34] to fully autonomous (e.g., Hungary).[35] In all reporting countries, the control of the proper authorization of the local budget expenditures was perhaps the primary objective of the audit.

What is audited exactly, just the municipality or other affiliated entities as well? This is the question of the subject of the audit. An analysis of the reporting countries revealed two viewpoints concerning this question. On the one hand, these off-budget units can be viewed as separate legal entities incorporated under the relevant commercial law.[36] In this case, the audit depends only on a decision of the board of directors, with no direct state involvement other than that of an ordinary shareholder participating in the board elections. On the other hand, even if an entity is incorporated under the commercial law, it can still be viewed as a part of the state assets and therefore subject to outside audit by a government office.[37]

The question of timing refers to the difference between an *a priori* and an *a posteriori* audit. In addition to the standard *a posterior* audit of budgeted activities, the countries were asked to give examples, if any, where *a priori* audits were used to evaluate programs before any commitments had been made. In as many words, all respondents indicated that the system for an *a posteriori* audit was still under development, without the added difficulties of attempting to implement an *a priori* audit requirement. The most positive response in this regard came from Estonia, which stated that: "The requirement for an *a priori* audit isn't prescribed by Estonian legislation. At the same time, the possibility is not excluded."[38] Do it if you want, but nobody else does.

In summary, the current state of the art in all responding countries is the traditional financial and compliance auditing, the effective implementation of which is hindered by an insufficient number of qualified professionals. Many respondents recognized the need to extend the scope of the audit in order to provide decision-makers with the information necessary to assess the performance of an organization or to evaluate the effectiveness of a program. In this regard, Hungary is representative of efforts being undertaken in this direction, with municipalities experimenting with both formula-based finance and program budgeting.[39] However, these attempts have so far been restricted to quantifiable parameters (e.g., students per teacher) and no attempts have been made to measure qualitative outputs of programs (e.g., quality of education). But these efforts are very much at the forefront, with the majority of respondents still struggling to implement the traditional audit function at the municipality level.

4. CONCLUSION AND RECOMMENDATIONS

As stated in the introduction, the purpose of this study has been to document the current state of Public Expenditures Management in eight CEE countries. For academic researches, this document is meant to provide descriptive data useful in the development of a theory of public finance as well as a framework for further research in the actual practices currently followed by government employees in the budgeting process. For practitioners, the study provides a starting point for knowledge transfer and system development. A careful review of systems and procedures existing in comparable countries will either confirm the appropriateness of, or provide a catalyst to changing, the current system.

The implicit proposition of the study has been that change in budgeting practices is necessary.[40] With change as the goal, the following standard management consulting model is useful to put the current study into perspective and provide a framework for future activities in each of the countries.[41]

Figure 3.5
A Model for Best Practice Transfer

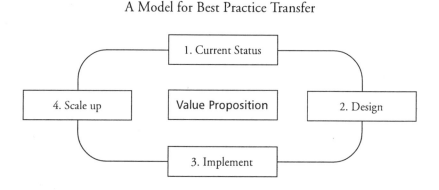

The starting point for all further activities is a clear statement of the value proposition (what do we want to become?) and a self-assessment of the current status of the system (where are we today?). The current study raised these questions, provided preliminary answers, and established a framework for refining the description in future research. The next stages in the change process, in outline form, will be:

- *Design*: What are the roles and functions of the people involved and what resources are available?
- *Implementation*: How can the ideas be tested on a smaller scale before being introduced into the whole system?
- *Scale Up*: What steps are necessary to implement the new ideas system wide?

Given that all countries included in the study have only relatively recently began to implement significantly different budgeting practices than were used in the past, it is too early to develop a list of "best practices." However, as a result of the continual evaluation of new procedures and organizational structures being tested in these countries, it has been possible for the study writers to provide recommendations concerning what does and does not work. A compilation of general recommendations made in a majority of reporting countries follows.

4.1 Decentralization

The process of decentralization should be continued and accelerated with respect to:
- *Spending authority,*
- *Taxing authority,*
- *Management of debt and guarantees,*
- *Reliable funding from central sources.*

"The *decentralization of management and budgeting responsibility* generally leads to the gradual improvement in the quality of financial plans, the reduction of the distance between decision-making and execution, and an increase in the flexibility of both planning and execution. Another very important result of this system is that it renders the complex decision-making process concerning the allocation of resources more objective."[42]

"Municipalities are unable to establish creditworthiness as a precondition for access to credit. A key prerequisite for the establishment of a municipal credit system is that *municipalities demonstrate creditworthiness*. This means that municipalities must show that they have the resources and willingness to repay debt. The current system of municipal finance works against this objective. The vast majority of municipal revenues comes from central government transfers, either shared taxes or subsidies. These are totally outside the control or influence of the municipalities."[43]

"All local units should be obligated to keep registers (off-balance sheet) of *guarantees* issued. It is necessary to keep special auxiliary records about guarantees that have been made. On the basis of the instructions of the central government, local units plan a guarantee reserve. However, in the instructions it is necessary to determine what amount (i.e., percentage) of the guarantees should be set aside in the guarantee reserve."[44]

"We can conclude that the main objective in terms of *revenue adequacy and control* is to ensure adequate revenues to fund the operating and capital costs of mandated and local discretionary services. For mandated services, the underlying principle is that central transfers will cover the operating costs of mandated services at a basic, adequate level. For discretionary services, the main principle is that municipal governments should have sufficient local revenue-raising authority and control to fund the level of services that the local community desires and is willing to pay for. This means that flexibility must be built into the local revenue structure such that individual municipalities will have the ability to raise differing amounts depending on local priorities."[45]

4.2 Expenditures

- *The list of services to be provided by local government should not be changed during a budget year.*
- *Local governments must develop systems to be able to estimate more accurately the cost of providing services.*

"This lack of clarity in service assignment not only creates confusion but also invites misuse of authority by central ministries. That is, central ministries can shift mandates onto municipal government at will—and often without legislative authority—since there is no legal barrier. Indeed, the concept of shared responsibility invites such abuse."[46]

4.3 Funding Predictability

- *The central transfer system should be simplified and not modified during the budget year.*

"The *responsibilities of the local public administrations,* and implicitly the related expenditures, should be established permanently, so that medium- and even long-term financial planning would also be possible. In the case of a transfer of responsibilities, the normative act should very clearly indicate the respective revenue source."[47]

4.4 Capital Expenditures

- *Modern capital budgeting evaluation techniques should be introduced.*
- *Systems should be developed in order to enter into multi-year commitments to fund investment projects.*

"Certain budget appropriations should be defined which are not voted on annually (e.g., *long-term contracts, debt repayment*). Naturally the budget would provide information to the decision-makers about the amounts, with the budget clearly showing these obligations separately from the discretionary spending, thus indicating that any potential delay in the approval of the budget would not impede making payments on these commitments."[48]

"The *system of municipal investments* should be adjusted to meet the requirements necessary to enable the local government to receive funds from the programs of the European Union. Various public channels, through which external investment funds could be obtained, should be integrated. It should be possible to consider the resources of local governments as well as the support grants from the State as joint financing sources with respect to applications for structural funds from the European Union. The Ministry of Internal Affairs has also suggested that resources should be allocated from the State budget in accordance with the project-principle for the entire period of an investment project."[49]

4.5 Budgeting Process

- *Recognize that local government budgeting requirements differ from those at the central level and allow for variations in local government budget preparation and presentation.*
- *Gradually move in the direction of accrual-based budgeting.*

"It seems that *over-regulation* is one of the most important problems in municipal budgeting. While the municipal system leaves the municipalities almost absolutely unconstrained, the public finance system contains many unnecessary requirements that reduce the flexibility of the municipality to adjust the local budget to fit the local requirements. The number of regulations concerning municipal budgeting, especially about the information contained in the budget document, should be reduced. Currently, the local budget document includes much information that is not of interest to the local politicians or that is not directly relevant for the local budget (e.g., the expenditures following a rigid classification system). Naturally, according to the rules, the municipal budget can contain other information in addition to that defined by central requirements, but in this case the budget containing both requirements becomes unwieldy."[50]

"It is recommended that the Ministry of Finance should promulgate revised accounting and financial reporting standards that end budget development and budget execution reporting on a cash-basis. In its place, municipalities should be required to adopt a method of accounting that, at a minimum, formally recognizes accounts payable as an obligation that must be liquidated within the current budget year. Such a system is termed 'cash plus commitments' or 'cash plus encumbrances'. Under commitment accounting, municipalities would record expenditure obligations when they were incurred rather than when paid. This change would force recognition of unpaid bills as an obligation payable from the budget."[51]

4.6 Human Resources

- *Introduce training in accrual accounting, budgeting and capital investment evaluation to a broad segment of government employees involved in the budgeting process.*

"Our research has proven the hypothesis that the local offices are not aware of the policy in other, even neighboring, municipalities. There are many cases where the municipalities in one area face problems that have already been resolved in other areas, but the solutions are not disseminated. Because municipal associations are very weak in Hungary, the central government and its field offices must play a central role in arranging this information exchange. As some examples (e.g., the treasury system or the program budgeting used in budgeting the central investment program) indicate, the local governments are ready to follow the centrally used or suggested methods, especially if the central budget contains 'incentive funds' and conditional grants for covering a part of the implementation costs."[52]

4.7 Planning

- *Introduce a system to explicitly link the budget process with long-term strategic plans for the provision of services and investment projects.*

"There is a lack of *correspondence between the funding and the usage* of key mandated services. Many municipalities provide services, particularly schools and social care facilities that have strong spillover effects. However, the funding for these services does not recognize the nature of the inter-jurisdictional costs. In the past, the Ministry of Finance attempted to adjust the municipal subsidy on the basis of recognizing differences in facilities usage and certain groups of dependent populations. However, these so-called 'objective criteria' are no longer used in the subsidy formulation and, in fact have steadily been losing their weighting in the formula over the past several years."[53]

"Indeed, as we have repeatedly stressed, the weakest aspect of the Polish budgeting system lies in its indifference to the costs of providing services and its failure *to link the costs of services with their output*. This results in the inefficient management of human and financial resources, the arbitrary and uninformed evaluation of work and personnel and work that is itself unfocused and unclear."[54]

4.8 Asset Management

- *Introduce long-term capital planning.*
- *Introduce and maintain accurate asset registers.*

"It is necessary to introduce into the procedure of *planning capital investments* the practice of making investment studies including the consideration of possible sources of financing. Since this concerns projects that are important for society as a whole, the obligation to make a social justifiability study of each investment should be imposed."[55]

"Local governments and their subsidiary units are also required *to inventory and value the public property* they own or administer and to submit to the Ministry of Finance and the RIO's consolidated balance sheets that summarize their assets and liabilities. Thus, in theory, local governments should have reasonable information about the value of their assets. In practice, however, this is rarely the case and the asset value data contained in these balance sheets is considered too unreliable to be of much use."[56]

4.9 Transparency and Publicity

- *Make the audit process more regular and clearly scheduled.*
- *Introduce elements of performance measurement and strategic information into the system.*
- *Develop formats for presenting the budget to interested citizens in a way that is more easily understood.*

"In most local governments, the audit committee of the Council is the only unit that carries out the internal control function. The work of the audit committee should become more *regular and clearly scheduled*. This would enable it to control all budget units within a predetermined time period. In smaller communities, the internal control could be jointly contracted out to regional development centers."[57]

"*Internal control* is not organized at either the ministry or the local level. Therefore, an internal control system should be set up in larger local units and used to provide an audit function to smaller units that are incapable of doing this themselves."[58]

"The annual budget, with its classification of objects by expenditure along with the related accounting, reporting, control and audit systems, should be improved. In the long run, these systems should be converted into a *performance-based system* that allows managers and accountants to utilize both service performance and accounting data."[59]

"To increase *citizen involvement*, a citizen's guide (the budget in brief) to the local budget should be prepared. It would explain what the budget is, how it is formulated, where the revenues come from and how they are spent, how pay categories are determined, how block grants are allotted by the central government, how the local budget and central government budget processes interrelate, and finally and most important what the role of the citizen is and how each individual can contribute."[60]

NOTES

[1] See Fisher, Irving, *The Theory of Interest*, (New York: Augustus M. Kelley, Publishers, 1965). Reprinted from the 1930 edition. The Fisherian model has provided the micro-foundations for much of the modern theory of aggregate consumption and saving by households. See, for example, the following: Friedman, Milton: *A Theory of the Consumption Function*, (Princeton, N.J.: Princeton University Press, 1957).

[2] Arrow, Kenneth J.: *Social Choice and Individual Values*, (John Wiley and Sons, Second Edition, 1963).

[3] For example, by March in the case of Estonia or July in the case of Albania.

[4] See Estonia, section 2.4.2., for a detailed description of this process.

[5] Albania, section 2.5.

[6] Bulgaria, section 2.6.

[7] Hungary, section 2.5.

[8] cf. Hungary, section 2.5.

[9] Hungary, section 2.10.

[10] Estonia, section 2.5.

[11] For a comprehensive description of these functions, see Musgrave, Richard A.: *The Theory of Public Finance*, (New York: McGraw-Hill, 1959).

[12] The difficulty of discussing budgeting as a policy process lies basically in the difference between discussing private sector companies or individuals and

government budgeting. For an in depth discussion of this idea, see Hőgye, Mihály: *Theoretical Approaches to Public Budgeting*, in Chapter 1.

[13] Cf. Albania, section 2.4., which lists and describes in detail the following: the city council, the head of the local government, the permanent economic and finance commission, the financial office of the local government, the heads of other departments, the civil society organizations, citizens and even international non-government organizations operating in Albania.

[14] Poland, section 2.4.

[15] Poland, section 2.4. For wonderful examples of pioneering efforts to involve their citizens in the budgeting process, see the examples given in the chapter.

[16] Horngren and Foster; "*Cost Accounting: A Managerial Emphasis*," 6th edition, (Prentice-Hall; p. 833).

[17] Russia, section 2.7.2.

[18] Russia, section 2.7.2.

[19] Bulgaria, section 2.8.

[20] Croatia, section 2.6.

[21] The authors, of course, at this point would like to claim that the research design was guided by prescience of the current corporate scandals such as Enron involving the use of such structures to hide important information from outsiders. Unfortunately, this is not the case.

[22] Estonia, section 2.3.

[23] Croatia, section 2.3.5.

[24] "Heads I win, tails you lose."

[25] Albania, section 2.3.

[26] The reader is referred to developments in such topics as Just-In-Time (JIT), Total Quality Management (TQM), Computer Integrated Manufacturing (CIM), and Decision Support Systems (DSS), which did not exist 40 years ago and are now mainstream topics in business schools.

[27] *Management Control Systems, 9th Edition*; Robert, N. Anthony and Vijay Govindarajan, (McGraw-Hill Publishing, 1998).

[28] Bulgaria, section 2.4.

[29] Hungary, section 2.4.

[30] Poland, section 2.5.

[31] Cf. Hungary, section 2.4.

[32]   Croatia, section 2.9.

[33]   Albania, section 2.9.

[34]   Russia, section 2.4. As an example of central control with an extreme element of uncertainty in the authorization system, no better example can be cited. For an example of how uncertainty can be cascaded down through the system from top to bottom, while at the same time allowing local officials to legally disburse funds despite the absence of an accepted budget, it is instructive to read these two pages of the country study.

[35]   Hungary, section 2.9. "There is no requirement for authorizing any part of the local budget by a central agency. Naturally, the central level attempts to ensure that the municipal budget complies with the few regulated points. The main tool for this is the authorization by the municipal external auditor."

[36]   See Hungary, section 2.9. "But the municipal companies are not part of the public finance system—they are incorporated under private law. The result is that the audit of the companies depends only on a decision by the Board of Directors."

[37]   See Estonia, section 2.9. "The State Audit Office is an independent budget organization set up to ensure the appropriate utilization and management of State assets. In addition to State assets, it provides a control function in enterprises in which the State has a majority share."

[38]   Estonia, section 2.9.

[39]   Hungary, section 2.4.

[40]   In none of the responses was there any discussion of the need for change. The implicit assumption that change is necessary in order to better allocate available resources and thus better satisfy the wants of the constituents was not questioned.

[41]   This typical consulting model is taken from O'Dell, Carla and C. Jackson Grayson, Jr.: "*If Only We Knew What We Know,*" (Free Press, 1998).

[42]   Poland, section 2.4.

[43]   Bulgaria, section 2.4.

[44]   Croatia, section 2.11.

[45]   Bulgaria, section 2.3.

[46]   Bulgaria, section 2.2.1.

[47]   Romania, section 2.2.

[48]   Hungary, section 2.

[49]   Estonia, section 2.5.

[50] Hungary, section 2.

[51] Bulgaria, section 2.5.1.

[52] Hungary, section 2.

[53] Bulgaria, section 2.1.1.

[54] Poland, section 2.2.

[55] Croatia, section 2.18.

[56] Poland, section 2.7.

[57] Estonia, section 2.7.

[58] Croatia, section 2.12.

[59] Albania, section 2.

[60] Albania, section 2.

Annex: Terms of Reference
For the Local Government Budgeting Project

Ákos Szalai

PART I.
LOCAL GOVERNMENT SYSTEM

1. Local Government Structure

The comparative study will need some basic information about: (i) the history and (ii) the current structure of the municipal system. This short introduction should answer some basic issues:

1. Legislative Background of the Municipal System
   Questions: *Does the constitution contain guarantees for municipal (local government) rights? Does law on municipalities exist? Does the modification of this act require a specific parliamentary process or is this similar to other acts? What were the most important steps in creating municipal systems? What were the main modifications since the "birth of the municipal system?" Is there any plan for further changes?*

2. Main Characteristics of the Municipal System
   Questions: *How many tiers exist? What is the relation between the different levels? The senior level can influence the local policies, or on the contrary? How? Is there any difference in the local municipalities? Does the capital or some major towns have specific rights? Are there any differences among the functions or revenues, etc., of the rural and the urban municipalities? What are the main points of these differences?*

3. Size of the Municipalities
   Questions: *How large are the municipalities? What is their average number of inhabitants (according to the legal types of the municipalities, e.g., local vs. regional/county level, major cities, urban vs. rural, etc.)? Is there any plan to "rationalize" the municipal system (e.g. reducing the number of municipalities, creating new tiers, or to reforming the system in any other way)?*

4. Role of Central Government in Providing Local Services
    Questions: *What are the local and regional units of national government in providing public services? Which service responsibilities are shared between central and local governments?*

5. Special Bodies
    Questions: *Are there any special purpose bodies, special districts, etc., which are not treated as part of the municipal system, but have regional or local authority in specific fields?*

Central Control over Municipalities

The central government always keeps some control over the municipalities. This control can be analyzed in two dimensions: (i) the target of the control and (ii) the institutional form. The country studies should concentrate only on control over the municipal budget and the budget-making process.

Targets

Following OECD (1997), we differentiate two goals of control over sub-national systems.
  (a) Administrative control. This is the classical goal of central governments; they want to ensure that the operation of lower tiers is legal and regular.
  (b) Performance-based evaluation. This kind of appraisal concentrates on five economic and social questions: Whether the local policies are: (i) relevant, (ii) effective, (iii) efficient, (iv) sustainable and (v) help institutional development.
Questions: *What are the main goals of the central control; with what tools do they reach these goals?*

Institution

Concerning the institutions for controlling sub-national tiers, the countries can be divided into two groups: the system is based either (i) on agencies or (ii) on prefects.
  (i) Deconcentrated administration. In this system many field offices monitor the operation of lower levels. Each ministry involved in local affairs has its own agency. These field offices are equal to each other, and they are responsible only to the ministry concerned.
  (ii) Prefect system. The prefects are the "heads" of the state administration at territorial level. In this system weak hierarchical links exist between this office and other state agencies.
Questions: *The country studies, besides a short description of the whole system, should concentrate on the local budget-making process: which agencies have an effect on*

budgeting (e.g., regional public accounting offices, etc.), what tools do these agencies (or the prefect) have in this field (e.g., a prior approval for the whole or for some parts of the budget, etc.)?

State Treasury

In countries where the state treasury exists, generally this has a great effect on the local budget-making process (e.g., in France, the state treasury includes the municipalities as well, so independent municipal cash management does not exist).

Questions: *Does a central treasury exist? What is its effect on local budgeting? Does this keep the municipal account, does this transfer the central grants to municipalities, does this make a part of or the whole municipal accounting, etc.?*

Cooperation among Levels of Government

The strong connection among the different levels can help in: (i) clarifying the national goals (e.g. this process can prevent sub-national policies running against the objective of macro-stability), (ii) involving sub-national sources (e.g. the expenditures at different levels can be harmonized and concentrated to particular goals), (iii) information flow. In some countries the municipalities (or the associations of municipalities) play a great role in the vertical distribution of public revenues among different tiers (e.g., proposed modifications in the system have to be approved by federal-state-municipal committees, or by the second chamber of the parliament which consists of the representatives of the municipalities, etc).

Question: *What is the role the municipalities (their associations) have in the central budget-making process, especially in the decisions on the vertical distribution of funds?*

2. Local Politics and Administration

As budgeting is one of the main activities of the organizations of local governments, the international comparison should consider the differences in the internal structure of the local governments.

We formed three groups from these issues:

1) *Executive Power*
   Municipalities, by definition, have elected "deliberative bodies." The functions of these bodies are similar to parliament, they have to pass local regulation, by-laws, etc. However, a government or president must exist at municipal level as well. This would be the mayor, and his or her staff, or may have a corporate body (e.g., in the

largest Danish municipalities, these bodies consist of the mayor and five to seven other people elected by the municipal body). These organizations are responsible for formulating options, "bills," for deliberative bodies, and these executive bodies are the first control over the administration.

Questions: *Are there separate executive bodies in the municipalities? And, if yes, how does the central legislation regulate its role in the budget-making process? Who is responsible for creating a budget proposal for the deliberative body?*

2) *Committee System*

Generally, the deliberative bodies have rights to create committees for helping the work of elected representatives in specific policies and for involving specific knowledge from outside the municipalities. The formulation and the basic rights of these committees are regulated in central legislation in many countries (e.g., the Hungarian Law on Local Self-Government requires that middle-sized and large municipalities have to set up financial committees which have to form opinion about the budget proposals, and have to control the financial activities of the local governments.)

Questions: *How does central legislation regulate the formulation and the functions of the municipal committees (if these exist)? What are the main effects of these regulations on the budget-making process and local budgeting?*

3) *Structure of Municipal Administration*

As the local bureaucrats have to administer the local policies and the local budgets, the central regulations on the differing structures of municipal administration are crucial comparisons.

Questions: *Who is the head of municipal administration? What is his/her role in budget-making, what is the legal relation between him/her and the head of local financial administration? Is there any specific regulation on local financial administration? Are its roles in budget making regulated centrally? Does this depend only on the local decisions and/or of the head of municipal administration? Is there any professional/skill requirements for employees in the municipal financial administrations?*

3. Municipal Functions and Service Delivery

Local discretion

In order to compare the local budgeting in different countries, we need to know what tasks are in the hands of local government and how large the area of local discretion is.

Questions: *Country reports should analyze the local functions and the municipal freedom in different sectors. What are the legally defined municipal functions and how the central level limits the local discretion? The sectors, which have to be analyzed, are:*

1) *police;*
2) *education;*
3) *health;*
4) *social provision, welfare;*
5) *water/waste-water;*
6) *waste-management;*
7) *housing;*
8) *heating;*
9) *telecommunication;*
10) *other sectors if they have a large share in local functions.*

NOTE: We have left out public administration from this list, because this area is very complex and analysis of this would require a very extensive report.

Differences according to the size/type of the municipalities
Questions: *In case the municipal system contains more types of local governments, then the differences in task allocation among the different types should be presented.*

Macro-economic control over the municipal policies
Many economists oppose decentralization because of the dangers to macro-economic stability. They state that the stabilization function should be kept at the central level, because the central level has enough resources for anti-cyclical (stabilization) policies. The main fears are that sub-national governments may: (i) create extra debt or deficit and (ii) impede fulfillment of national expenditure goals (e.g., they cause changes in the composition of the structure of expenditures, or the concentration of the resources for the main investment program is more difficult if the responsibilities are divided among many actors) and that (iii) municipalities may raise overall demand and cause deficits in the balance of payments.
Questions: *What are those central policies which aim to impede these macro-economic problems? How does the central government limit municipal borrowing? How do they try to avoid the shift from the centrally required investment/consumption share? How does the central level constrain the growth of public sector revenues/expenditures?*

4. Local Government Finances and Financial Management

Revenue Structure

One of the main indicators of the independence of municipalities is the high share of own-source revenue (small share of the central transfers) in the local budget.

Local Taxes

Local tax forms

The most frequently mentioned own-source revenue is local tax. Local taxes have many forms. The OECD statistics differentiate seven main forms:
  (a) municipalities set tax rates and tax base;
  (b) municipalities set tax rates only;
  (c) municipalities set tax base only;
  (d) revenue split, in which there is four sub-groups;
      (d1) municipalities determine revenue-split,
      (d2) revenue-split can only be changed with consent of municipalities,
      (d3) revenue-split fixed in legislation, may unilaterally be changed by central government,
      (d4) revenue-split determined by central government as part of the annual budget;
  (e) central government sets rate and base of municipal taxes.

The fiscal federalism (decentralization) literature frequently mentions the problems arising from harmful tax competition: the different tax rates on the mobile tax base (capital, income, etc.) encourage movement toward municipalities with lower tax rates. It can result in misallocation of factors or (if the local government must reduce the tax rate because of this inter-governmental competition) inefficiently low rates and public services. In the overlapping tax base, when more tiers levy tax on the same base, this tax competition can appear among the different tiers of government: a high tax rate at one level can reduce the tax base (e.g. through tax base emigration) and the tax revenues of the other tiers.

Question: *What tools does the central legislation employ against harmful tax competition (e.g., setting minimum and maximum local rates, defining only an immobile base for local taxation)?*

User Charges

The other main form of municipal revenues are user charges (including administration fees). According to the OECD definition, the main difference between taxes and user charges is that user charges are requited current revenues, while taxes are not.

Central limitation on local discretion
Questions: *What is the limitation on local discretion in a decision over user charges (e.g., defining the list of services, maximizing the amount, or regulating the calculation of the level of fees, charges)?*

Outsourcing tendencies
The issues of user charges is especially important if the privatization of local services is a strong tendency. In this case the functions for which the municipal budget formerly receives fees and charges move outside the municipal budget (e.g., the low share of user charges can be caused by the fact that functions have been privatized and these charges flow to private firms and not to the municipal budget).
Questions: *Are there strong privatization tendencies in local services? What services are typically privatized?*

Other Non-Tax Revenues

Besides the above mentioned own-sources, the local government can have other revenue sources, e.g., entrepreneurial income, fines/forfeits, contribution to municipalities within government, etc.
Questions: *Is there any central regulation concerning these revenue sources?*

Business function in local governments
In some countries the basis of the intergovernmental finance system is municipal property, and the revenues from these properties form a great part of municipal revenues. In this case (and in every case when the municipalities have entrepreneurial properties) one of the main tasks of the government is the efficient management of these properties.
Questions: *What is the value of the municipal properties (assets)? What central limitations exist on municipal property management? Are there special forms for municipal properties, like budgetary enterprise, or must all municipally owned firms run under the civil/commercial law?*

Intergovernmental grants to current budget

The international literature on intergovernmental grants differentiates three forms of transfers.

Unconditional (general) grants

The central government supports the municipalities without any condition concerning their use. This type of transfer gives the most autonomy to municipalities. Generally this form is employed for equalization among the municipalities.

Questions: *What are the main goals of these grants? How, and with the help of what formulae, are the funds of unconditional grants allocated / distributed among the municipalities (e.g., on a "per capita" base; on a "local need base" when the central level considers the potential expenditure need in the municipalities; on a "revenue capacity base," when the tax base of the local governments are considered; or on the philosophy of "equalizing fiscal effort" when the basis of the distribution is the differences between the estimated expenditure needs and the tax potential of the municipalities)?*

Conditional non-matching

The local governments must use this amount only for certain expenditures. This is an earmarked grant—it may be a specific grant for a specified program or a block-grant for a generally defined area. But its effect is smaller than the central government often expects, due to the fact that the municipality can reduce its own effort in the area of grants.

Questions: *What are the main targets (expenditures, functions) of this form of grants? Are there any central tools to impede the reduction of local efforts in the subsidized fields?*

Matching

The sub-national governments are required to contribute to the program—the central government gives a certain amount in grants for each unit of local expenditure. The typical form is partial cost reimbursement.

Vis major grants

Almost every intergovernmental financial system includes some forms of grants for the municipalities in financial trouble.

Questions: *Do these funds exist? How large are they and what are the criteria for achieving these funds?*

Financing these grants

The last question to be discussed in this section is financing the equalization system. Based on international experiences we can define two options.

(i) Financing from the inter-municipal fund. This uses negative equalization as well: the better-off localities are required to contribute to the fund. It could have disincentive effects, e.g., the local governments may not be interested in raising the local tax base.

(ii) Financing from the central budget. This method lifts the below-standard municipalities without reducing the revenues of the better-off entities.

Questions: *How are the grants financed, in general, and are there any important exemption (e.g., large elements of the grant system)?*

5. Capital Investment Financing and Capital Budgeting

Municipal investment can form a great part of overall investment and especially public sector investment. Municipal borrowing is also part of the overall public deficit. It is natural that the central government, which has the first responsibility over the macro-economic stability and growth, attempts to validate the macro-economic targets of the municipal budget as well.

Questions: *What central limitations exist on municipal capital spending and borrowing (e.g., limits on the amount of annual debt issuing or of total debt, approval from higher level for debt/investment, restricting long-term borrowing to capital expenditures, limitations on the amount and targets of capital spending, etc.)? Are municipalities allowed to go to the credit market, or there is a special institute fulfilling this task? Does the state provide subsidized loans for municipal capital investments? Do central funds (e.g. guaranty funds, revolving funds) exist for enhancing the municipal creditworthiness? This chapter should list the main central investment grants, with their: (i) targets, (ii) amounts, (iii) types (unconditional, conditional, matching), (iv) financing sources and other important features.*

PART II.
LOCAL GOVERNMENT BUDGETING (FISCAL PLANNING)

International experiences indicate that there are two main tendencies in the budgeting practice of developed countries. The governments attempt: (i) to allocate resources based on outputs/outcomes rather than on controlling inputs (performance budgeting), and (ii) to make budgets with a multi-year horizon. The main objective of the international comparison is to study whether the regulation in the partner countries requires, promotes or constrains that the municipalities introduce and employ these techniques. The municipal capacity for employing these techniques will be the subject of the second phase. The international comparison will concentrate on the key practices, which are required by these budgeting methods: accrual budgeting and accounting, global (vs. line-item) budget, performance measurement, etc.

1. Fiscal Policy-Making and Budgeting at National Level

The following pages will deal with the central regulation and central policies directly effecting local budgeting, but we also need other information on the central practices which have effects on the local budgets and budget-making. The most important effect can be this example: Hungarian municipalities often follow the central examples in many cases without explicit central regulation, or the information that the central government provides to municipalities may also have a large influence on municipal activities. Questions: *Who* are the actors, *what* are the subjects of planning, *how* is the national budget prepared, *when* is it prepared and presented? Only those aspects of fiscal planning at national level should be discussed that are significant for local government budgeting.

2. Strategic Planning and Short-Term (Annual) Budgeting at Local Level

The first step has only an indirect link with the budget-making process in a narrow sense —it is the formulation of political programs and policies. In most countries, a central requirement is the creation of such programs (either in the form of specific programs for sectors or of single-development plans). In many cases the financial department does not take part in this process, which causes many problems in budget-making.

Questions: *The country studies should list the centrally required long- or medium-term sectoral or general development programs and their main targets. How do the budgetary effects of the planned policies have to be presented in these documents? How does central policy regulate the role of budgetary/financial departments in this process?*

3. Basic Structure of Local Budget

This chapter deals with some basic issues of the required budget structure: (i) the issues of the fund system, (ii) off-budget units, (iii) extra-budgetary units and (iv) units of fiscal planning.

Fund System

Separation of capital and current budget: golden rule, operational deficit
Above, this TOR differentiates two parts of the budget: the current or operating and capital revenues, expenditures. Many countries (e.g., in the USA) separate these into "two budgets, two funds" and they attempt to constrain cross-financing between the two funds, e.g., through the "golden rule" when the central government forbids deficit in the current budget.

Questions: *How does the central regulation define the current and capital revenues/expenditures? (What revenues and expenditures are parts of the different funds?) Does the municipal budget have to formally separate the two funds or not? Is there any central policy to impede financing current expenditure from capital revenues? In case of separated funds, what is in the central regulation to ensure that the municipalities will consider the "current budget consequences" (e.g., the cost of maintenance in the next years) in any investment decisions?*

Earmarked funds
Almost every budget has special revenue streams that are earmarked, so they need to be handled separately. Theoretically, the public finance textbooks oppose the use of these earmarked funds, because these reduce the incentive to use them in a more efficient way. In practice, municipalities often violate these conditions and prohibitions.

Questions: *What funds are earmarked according to the central legislation, and what techniques does the central government employ to control the expenditure financed from these revenues? What revenues and expenditures are parts of these funds?*

Units of Fiscal Planning

Units in the budget
One of the most important issues of fiscal planning is what are the basic units of the budget. These would be municipal institutions (mayor's office, schools, hospitals, etc.), departments of the municipal office and municipal programs. The treatment of the municipal companies is crucial, especially for transparency of the budget, see next chapter).
Questions: *What type of fiscal units are parts of the municipal budget (e.g., municipal institutions, municipal companies, etc.)? Are the municipal companies parts of the local budget?*

Performance budget: planning at institutional or program level
As we mentioned, one main issue of our research will be the option of performance budgeting. The next parts will deal with budgeting techniques, but some basic public finance regulation could have negative effects on the options. The first of these is the requirements concerning the unit of fiscal planning. Many regulations require planning revenues and expenditures at institutional level, while performance budgeting would require assigning institutional costs to services and programs. This requires that the accounting and reporting method should deal with the cross-financing of the programs (e.g., when the first organization owns the asset and the other operates/manages the program using this asset).
Questions: *What is the required level of budgeting and accounting: institutions or programs? How does the public finance accounting system attempt to deal with the problems of cross-financing among institutions?*

Extra-Budgetary Funds, Off-Budget Units

Creating off-budget units and extra-budgetary funds
Every budget system provides options to form such public units (e.g., foundations, companies and non-profit organizations) that are not part of the budget. But the transparency and the efficiency of the public funds require that most revenues are parts of a single budget. Most public finance systems attempt to limit the freedom of the municipalities (and other parts of the system) in creating these separated units.
Questions: *How does the central government regulate the formulation of these off-budget units (in general and at municipal level especially)? In which cases do the municipalities have options to set up such units? And when is it required (e.g., how is the foundation of municipal companies regulated)?*

Consolidation of the budgets

One basic requirement in public budgeting is to present the extra-budgetary funds, items and assets as well, e.g., information on public enterprises, public institutions and non-profit organizations. Moreover, many municipalities support these units or receive dividends from them. The system of these transfers among the different units and between the units and the municipal budget (support, transfer or free use of municipal asset, dividend, investment on behalf of the municipality, etc.) is very complex.

Questions: *How does central government regulate creating, budgeting and accounting of extra-budgetary units? How are they to be incorporated into the municipal budget?*

Expenditure Classification

The main difference between the performance and the line-item budget is that the classical form basically focuses on the micro-control of expenditures, while the performance budget considers information on the performance of programs and services. Many experts see that the global budget is the synonym of the performance budget. The line-item budget provides exact division of expenditures among the different expenditure categories, while the global budget consists of one consolidated appropriation for all running cost. The further division of the cost in the programs is not part of the budget, but this is the responsibility of the program management. On the other hand many public finance systems require that the expenditures have to be classified into some defined lines (classes).

Questions: *What classification is required by central legislation? How do the municipalities have to divide their expenditures and revenues (current and capital as well), and how does the central regulation define the different expenditure and revenue categories?*

4. Budgeting Techniques

The traditional line-item budgeting considers only the input size of the services and institutions. In most cases this is based on the previous year's input (expenditure) level. It is well known that most countries employ these budgeting techniques. Generally, the central legislation contains explicit or implicit requirements which can be fulfilled if the local government uses the traditional incremental budgeting techniques: the previous year's expenditure has to be increased with the centrally required or locally accepted increase.

Questions: *Are there explicit central requirements for employing incremental, line-item budgeting techniques? Does the central level have such budget requirements (e.g., required nominal increases in some expenditure classes or in some sectors) that can be met only through line-item/incremental budgeting techniques?*

This chapter attempts to analyze other, new techniques: (i) performance budgeting, (ii) accrual budgeting and (iii) multi-year budgeting

Performance Budget—Role of Performance Indicators

According to the most accepted definition, performance budgeting means that there are budgetary consequences of the performance level. However, the link between the performance of the previous year's and next year's budget is very rarely direct. Generally, the effects of the performance indicators on the budget are influential: the ex-post evaluations play a great role in the negotiation phase when the budget officers and the managers of institutions set explicit output/outcome targets. These targets (the indicators of these targets) are incorporated into the budget documents. Based on these indicators, incentive systems can be set up for public sector managers, e.g., in the form of performance-related payments, either on an individual level (bonus for management) or on a group-basis. In many countries, e.g., New Zealand and Great Britain, this is a widely used, or obligatory, technique. Questions: *What performance indicators and information do the national policies require to be incorporated into the annual budget documents? Are there any legally defined consequences of good or bad performance, is there any centrally employed or offered incentive system? What performance information systems and what incentive policies exist at central level?*

Accrual (Cost-Based) Budgeting or Cash-Based Budgeting

While most budgets are based on the cash principle, some countries (e.g., Australia, New Zealand, Great Britain and the Netherlands) change the focus of budget-making to the cost principle. The international organizations (OECD, World Bank) also suggest accrual (or modified accrual) budgeting as the key element for implementing performance budgeting. In case of accrual budgeting and accounting, the revenues are recorded when they are earned not when received, and expenditures are recorded when liability is incurred not when paid. The accounting of investment is also different in the two systems. Accrual accounting, similar to private sector accounting, spreads these costs during the useful life of the asset (through depreciation), while the cash budget records the whole expenditure in the year of investment. However, it is well known that there are two main problems with this new method of budgeting and accounting. First the accrued revenues (e.g., accrued tax) are not fully received. The solution to this problem would be modified accrual accounting, when only the expenditure side is accounted and budgeted on an accrual basis, while the revenue side remains on a cash basis. Secondly, some international requirements (e.g., the Maastricht Treaty and Pact for Stability and Growth) require information based on cash, not accrual, accounting.

Questions: *What are the basic accounting principles in municipal budgeting, and what differences are between these and the principles for private sector accounting?*

Multi-year, Guaranteed Budget

There are some programs requiring multi-year contracts for service delivery, or for construction. The "pure form of performance budgeting" uses "sunset regulation" for these programs: they should achieve the agreed goals (effects) by the end of this period. On the other hand there are many programs which have cross-budget-year effect. Some current expenditure programs (e.g., raising the salary of public employees) have effects on the next year's budget.

Question: *What information must be in the budget document concerning the multi-year effect of the expenditures and revenues (not only the capital budget)?*

5. Participants and Actors in Local Government Planning

Budget-making is primarily a policy process, and is maybe the most important policy decision taken by the municipality. This process is a "many-player-game," in which almost each service department, every institution, all lobbies and local political parties and other pressure groups take part. The financial department and the head of the municipality (mayor, vice mayor, CAO/CFO) play the most important roles in this process. They have to deal with claims from the line-departments and lobbies, they have to find a balance between these demands, but also they have to protect the interests of the "whole population" against the lobbies. Many countries centrally identify the most important social groups and lobbies and create institutions for negotiation among them.

Questions: *What central requirements govern negotiations in the preparatory phase (who has to participate, what are the main subjects of this negotiation, etc.)? What are the legally defined roles of: (i) the local politicians, (ii) the finance and service departments, (iii) the service organizations and (iv) the general public and civic organizations?*

6. Major Stages of Budgeting

The textbooks differentiate five main stages of the budgeting cycle: preparation, approval, modification, implementation and reporting. Legislation in most countries sets up a detailed timetable for the budgeting period. Generally, in these timetables, some dates are defined exactly (e.g., up to which day the municipal budget proposal or the reports

89

have to be submitted to the municipal bodies), but some actions are required in case of special situations, e.g., when the modification should be submitted.

Questions: *The country studies should present the budget calendar of municipalities and of those tiers which give grants for municipal budgets (including the required list and date of financial presentations). How does the central level define the main actions for each phase? What special situations are defined when budget modifications have to be submitted?*

Publicity

The budget document and the performance measurement (and assessment) system should contain information not only for local politicians, but for local voters as well. However, the legally required budget documentation is very complex. There are wide differences among the countries in the potential role of direct democracy in the budget-making process. Some countries forbid the use of public referendum in this process. Conversely, some constitutions, e.g., in some Swiss cantons, specific programs, especially investment programs and municipal borrowing, must be approved by local referendum.

Questions: *The country studies should contain those central legislation and central examples which attempt to make the budget documentation more understandable for voters. How does the central level regulate the role of the local inhabitants in the budget-making process (e.g., referendum, public hearing and publication of the short format of the budget in local media)?*

7. Information Systems

The information system includes: (i) the collection at local level, (ii) information gathering in national systems and (iii) dissemination among local governments. However, the structure of this chapter follows another logic—the type of information: fiscal (financial) and performance information.

Fiscal Information in Budget Documentation

The budget proposal is prepared for politicians and the local community; therefore it should include all necessary information to assess efficiency, effectiveness and fairness (e.g., whether the budget finances the different policies and programs to an acceptable level). Theoretically, the budget should contain explicit information on: (i) priorities, (ii) major changes from the current year and factors leading to changes, (iii) services to be provided and how these services are financed. Moreover, the budget should: (iv) aggregate expenditure according to various dimensions: object class (e.g., payroll, supplies, equipment, etc.); agencies (may also include program, sub-program, project and activity); functional categories (e.g., health, education, income support, etc.) and economic classification (e.g., purchases, transfers to individuals, net interest, etc.).

Questions: *What information is required to be in budget and how does the central policy ensure that these documents will be available to the public? What information about the budget and financial reports has to be sent to the agencies of central government and which will form part of the national statistical information?*

Performance Information   -

The traditional audit focused on financial transactions, but now its focus is on performance. The auditing standards of INTOSAI (International Organization of Supreme Audit Office) explicitly state, "The full scope of governmental auditing includes … performance audit" (Paragraph 38). While analyzing the performance measurement, we will concentrate only on two key issues of the performance information (audit) system: (i) the measurement and (ii) the criteria used for assessment.

Measurement

Performance measurement should indicate the efficiency and effectiveness of local programs and should provide useful information for decision-making (both for institutional managers and for budget-makers): This requires adequate, but in number and complexity limited, data and analytical tools for assessing the results. The basic data can be gathered from the official reporting system—the institution is obliged to provide information to the municipality or to the local community. Considering this source, the main issues are: (i) who must provide (ii) what information and (iii) to whom. The other option for gathering performance data is the public survey.

Questions: *What performance data do the municipalities have to collect and report for statistical offices or other governmental agencies, and what do the local budgets have to contain? How often must data be reviewed?*

Assessment

In many cases there are no well-defined benchmarks for the different public services. In order to avoid voluntaristic goal setting, the municipality should be based on intertemporal and intergovernmental comparisons.

Questions: *What roles do the central agencies or municipal associations or other organizations have for providing benchmarking to the municipalities?*

8. Budget Implementation

According to the Call for Proposal, the research will concentrate mainly on the issues of cash management; there will not be enough time to study the other elements of financial management, e.g., debt management, the procurement process or implementing capital (infrastructure) investment, etc. (See the next chapter on Capital Budgeting)

Cash Management Practices

While we use the word "management," the main question in the field researches will be do the municipalities have "management," "administration" or "bureaucracy." The main differences is in the focus of their activity. The administration has a legal purpose, e.g., financial administration must ensure that expenditures (and revenues) are consistent with the limits established in the local budget. The managerial purpose is to promote efficiency and effectiveness of local public finance.

Centralization of cash management: treasury system vs. management autonomy
According to the definition in OECD: "The main task of most governmental cash management systems is to ensure that the right amount of cash is available, at the right time, for the lowest possible cost." The main element here is forecasting, because if this is accurate, the overall amount of borrowing can be reduced through offsetting agencies' surpluses and needs against each other. Cash management has two opposite forms: centralization in the treasury system and decentralization based on management autonomy. In many countries the municipalities centralize their cash management, terminate the financial independence of the budgetary units and operate the cash flow through a single-account system. The main reasons are the greater specialization (and concentration) of knowledge, the simplicity of balancing the peaks and shortage of individual agencies, higher interest payment for short-term (e.g., overnight) investment and special bank conditions for any large amount in one account. However, performance management may require other methods for financing the activity of the institutions. It is generally accepted that if managers expect to be accountable for their performance, they must have decision-making authority and must be aware of the cost of the activity. "Cash-performance" is a good indicator of the performance of management.
Questions: *How does the central government help or impede the "single-account system" at municipal level, e.g., are separate accounts for certain state transfers or for different own source revenues required centrally? How large autonomy over cash does the central regulation require the institutional management to have?*

Investment policy for surplus funds and short-term borrowing
Municipalities should have policies for cases when the mentioned cash forecasting expects surplus funds or excess cash requirements. These policies have double goals: ensuring the maximum return (minimum loss) and minimizing the risk of insufficient cash at the time of the immediate cash needs.

Questions: *The case studies should concentrate on the centrally defined criteria: Does central government regulate in which financial institute, in which form and with which criteria (interest, term, etc.) the municipalities keep their surplus funds? Is there any central policy concerning the autonomy of the managers of the budgetary institutions in this field?*

Controlling the Budget of Service Organizations
(Expenditures and Own-Revenues)

The municipal services are provided by more or less independent units: in- or off-budget municipal units, public-private-partnership, etc. Financial information about these units is crucial, because the financial activities of the in-budget units are parts of the whole budget, and the bad (financial and service) performance in off-budget units could appear suddenly as a large claim against the municipal budget (e.g., consolidation, re-capitalization of firms).

Management authority in budget-making
In our opinion, the key difference between performance and line-item budgeting is the institutional and management autonomy to determine the mix of operational costs, and to make mid-year changes in the budget. Program management is responsible for the efficiency and effectiveness of the programs, so they have to have autonomy for dividing the expenditure into categories, for shifting expenditure among the lines and for using freely from efficiency gains.

Questions: *How large is the degree of management autonomy in budget-making? What role do the managers of the budgetary institutions have to play in budget-making (e.g., they have to accept the budget, etc.)? What opportunities do they have for shifting expenditures (and revenues) among categories, what mid-year changes may they make and what autonomy do they have over the end-of-year surplus?*

Expenditure: proper authorization for disbursement
The other side of management autonomy must be control over the spending level in order to avoid financial mismanagement, deficit and over-spending (e.g., in case of enlarging the expenditure side without sufficient revenues). Efficient cash management requires the disbursements to be based on proper authorization. The form of this authorization

process is linked to the (de)centralization of cash management. In the extreme case of centralization, explicit prior approval from the municipal office is often required for commitment. Naturally, the only requirement in decentralized management systems is that the institutions and departments do not exceed the budget limit. This budget limit can be annual or can be apportioned over quarters or months.

Question: *What is the centrally required disbursement mechanism?*

Audit System

Audit can be defined as a system which answers the question of "what we did and how." The main parts of this process, the performance and compliance audit, were analyzed in other parts of the study. This chapter deals with: (i) the auditor, (ii) authorization, (iii) the subject of and (iv) the time of audit.

Auditor

There are two basic forms of audit: internal and external audit. In most countries, the state audit office has responsibility for auditing the municipalities either through creating a separate audit office only for municipal audit or through the central office.

Questions: *Are there requirements on the internal audit? In which case do the municipalities have to hire an external auditor? What function does the state audit office have in the municipal audit? Is there a separate state audit office for municipalities? Does the state audit office prepare performance audits as well, or only compliance audits?*

Authorization

One of the most important functions of the municipal audit (either in the case of the budget, or in the case of municipal enterprises) is the authorization of the municipal activities and local budgets.

Questions: *Is there central regulation which requires that the municipal budget must be authorized? Which institution(s) have the right to authorize the municipal budget and reports? In case of no authorization, how does the central government attempt to ensure that the data in local budgeting activity is legal (compliance audit) and effective (performance audit)?*

Subject of audit

As we mentioned, in case the municipalities have off-budget units, their mismanagement can result in great problems in the municipal budget as well.

Questions: *Do these public units or municipally owned companies have special audit regulations? What are the differences between the audit of private firms and their own? In which case, how frequently do these have to be audited?*

Time of audit
In most cases the audit is made after the action (*a posterior*), but can also be before (*a priori*). Some public finance regimes define those situations when the auditor should audit the activity before or parallel to the actions.

Question: *Are there any cases defined in budgetary regulation when the municipality has to make an a priori audit?*

9. Capital Budgeting

Capital budgeting is one of the largest themes in budgeting literature. However, because of the limited time of this program we selected only some important points of this very important subject: (i) size of local capital investments, (ii) separation of current and capital funds, (iii) sources of capital budgets: national, local and external, and (iv) capital planning method. Some very important issues have to be left out, e.g., the implementation process, project management (public procurement, contracting, financing–borrowing, debt management, etc.) and the alternative service delivery options (privatization, concession, contracting-out, regulation on the private service provider, etc.). The first three of the aforementioned four issues of this research are analyzed formerly, either in Part I or in the earlier chapters of Part II. This chapter concentrates only on the methods (the steps) of capital planning and the issue of forecasting, which is generally one of the main impediments to appropriate planning.

Capital Planning Methods

It is generally accepted that formal links between planning and budgeting should be established and the (capital) budget of the municipalities should be set up on the basis of medium- or long-term development plans and programs. In the process of capital budget-making, three key points can be defined. Because municipal investments can receive capital grants from a central level in almost every country, *this chapter should concentrate not only on the legal requirements but on the incentives in the grants system (the preconditions of the central transfers) as well.*

1) *Establishing long-term development plans, based on defined goals of the local community (goals of governing politicians) and information about the current situation of the infrastructure and other assets.* Realistic development plans can not be set up if there is no up-to-date list of existing capital infrastructure with age, condition and other important characteristics of each facility. This picture of the current situation should compare the goals for quantity and qualities of different services

using this infrastructure. Based on this information the municipality is able to define the gap (the required investments) and to prioritize needs.

Questions: *What central requirements exist concerning: (i) the inventory of existing capital and (ii) municipal planning methods (process, term, main priorities, etc.)? Do the municipalities have to present the balance sheet in the budgetary process, in budgetary documents or in reports? Are there any differences between the valuation of assets in the private sector and in the public sector (e.g., depreciation, reassessment period, etc.)?*

2) *Choosing the capital investment programs for medium term, based on the analysis of the budgetary forecasting and the effect of the programs.* Based on the long-term plans, the municipality should select and schedule those programs which can be implemented in the medium-term (Capital Investment Plan, CIP or "rolling budget"). The municipality should focus on the effects of the programs when selecting them. According to the textbook, two types of effects must be considered: (i) the budgetary (cost of the program, expected change in future operational cost) and (ii) social, non-pecuniary effects (e.g., with cost-benefit or cost-effectiveness analysis). Only those projects can be accepted where the positive effects of which exceed the costs in both analyses. After selecting the programs that have net social benefit, municipalities should forecast their own expenditures and revenues without the effects of the project and on this base the investment projects should be scheduled. This multi-year CIP should ensure that the annual revenues will be sufficient to finance the direct cost, i.e.,the repayment of debts (and depreciation, in case of accrual accounting) of the projects.

Questions: *What mechanisms do municipalities have to employ when they select the investment programs in order not to be against central legislation, and in order to have a greater chance to receive central capital grants (e.g., Are the municipalities required to use cost-benefit or cost-effectiveness analysis for each program? Do they have to pass multi-year, rolling budgets? Are the balance criteria for this multi-year budget defined centrally? What are the consequences of the lack of these requirements)? Does the central government define the key parameters of these mechanisms (e.g., discount rates for cost-benefit analysis, the value of some non-marketable goods, like risk, time, environmental facilities, etc.)?*

3) *Developing financial plans for the individual project.* When starting the project, the municipality should secure the liquidity for financing the project cost. They have to decide whether they will borrow the money from the capital market or whether they will raise their own-source revenues (i.e., taxes, user charges), etc.

Questions: *What planning process is required (e.g., who must take part in the process, who has veto right, etc.), and what are the required data for these plans? What are the consequences if the municipalities do not achieve these requirements?*

Revenue and Expenditure Forecasts

As we mentioned, revenue and expenditure forecasting are essential to create multi-year budgets, but the single-year budget also requires predicting next year's revenue and expenditure, especially if the central budget has not been passed at the time of the preparatory phase of the local budget, or when the economy changes unpredictably, (e.g., inflation rate is high). Additional problems can arise if the main own-source revenues are very sensitive to fluctuations in the local economy.

Questions: *What channels exist through which the central governments provide information on the expected economic changes?*

Index

Italicized items – in references, in appendix, footnotes

accountability, 6, 10–12, 147, 149, 181, 189, 249, 282–284, 310–311, 348, 355, 361, 387, 531

accounting, 5–6, 8, 23–25, 27–29, 32–38, *41,* 53, 61–62, 68, 70, *71,* 77, 84, 86, 88, 129, 131, 133, 135, 145, 147–149, 183–184, 221, 230, 234, 239, 241, 246–248, 250–251, 255, 257–259, 266, 268–269, *272,* 309–310, 313, 315–316, 325–326, 334, 337, 347–348, 356, 359, 366–367, 372, 376, 384, 389, *395,* 419, 426–428, 441, 443–444, 451, 456, 458, 459, *460, 463,* 493, 496, 504, 506–508, 550, 557

accrual accounting, 32–33, 38, 61–62, 68, 84, 88, 96, 313, 366–367, 384, 389, *395*

administration, local, 57, 110–111, 115, 118, 121–122, 124, 147, 149, 159–164, 177–178, 180, 182, 185, 193, 207, *210,* 219–220, 222, 224, 229, 240, 270, 280–281, 288, 301, 319, 334, 336–337, 342, 358, 404, 406, 407, 437, 441, 467. 469, 471–473, 477, 481–483, 487–490, 492, 494, 496–497, 500, 502, 504–506, 508–511, 513–514, 516–517, *518,* 523, 525, 528–532, 537, 545, 547, 555

assets, 48, 53, 58, 63, 69, *72,* 86–88, 113, 117, 121, 132, 184–185, 187, 191, 205, 232, 238–241, 247, 250–251, 253, 263–264, 267–268, *271,* 282, 289, 302–303, 309, 313, 316–317, *326–327,* 345, 353, 358, 364, 367, 376–377, 383–384, 386, 385, 409, 417, 419, 424, 428, 441, 445, *456, 459,* 469, 477, 484, 487, 495, 504, 506, 510, 512–515, 518–519, 535, 548

audit office, 22, 24, 34, 36, 50, 63, *72,* 91, 94, 135, 178–179, 181, 183, 190, 192, 195–196, *210,* 259, 221, 230, 254–255, 259, *271,* 299, 315, 317, 348, 381, *395,* 507

audit, financial, 25, 27, 33–35, 64, 147, 184, 297, 310, 317, 380, 476, 506, 544

  performance, 34, 37–38, 91, 94, 184, 381–382

  systems, 33, 35, 59, 70, 91, 145, 147, 184, 259, 266, 281, 315–316, 374, 380, 382, 506

auditing, 24–25, 27, 33–36, 38, 45, 48–49, 63, 91, 94, 149, 181–185, 259–260, 265–266, 297, 334, 348, 380–381, 442–443, 506, 560, 568

auditors, external, 34–35, *72,* 94, 307, 348, 370, 380–382

  internal, 34–35, *41,*94, 184, 305, 381, 495

authority, 5–7, 12, 29, 31, 48–52, 56–58, 61, 63, 65–66, 92–93, 107–108, 111–113, 118, 121, 124, 128–129, 132, 139–141, 144, 146, 149, *151,* 165, 176, 182, 186, 196, 198–199, 201–202, 207, 221, 223–224, 226, 230, 236, 246, 252–254,280–281, 313, 322, 335, 342, 354, 361, 388, 415, 417, 432–433, 440, 442–443, *455, 460–461,* 470, 476–477, 479–480, 489, 494, 500, 510–511, 513, 517–518, 525, 529–531, 540, 542, 551, 565, 568–569,

autonomy, local, 48, 108, 110, 129, 142, 146–147, 206, 277, 281, 285, 333, 339, 344, 361, 401, 470–471, 475–476, 529–530

  financial, 107, 113, 130, 139, 195, 378, 469–471, 481, 494, 508–509, 516, 528, 568

block grants, 70, 82, 120, 136, 138, 140, 150

borrowing, long-term, 83, 205, 230, 424, 541,

  short-term, 57, 93, 183, 230, 378, 422, 489, 541,

budget, approval process , 5–9, 12, 77, 129, 139, 552

  calendar, 5, 90, 150, 212, 429, 552

  implementation, 10–12, 56–57, 89, 134, 140, 143, 172, 180–182, 217, 223, 231, 241, 243, 253–256, 258, 305, 313, 317, 331it, 372, 375, 382, 399, 440, 447, *457,* 523, 557, 560

  classification, 50–51, 70, 130, 131, 144, 147, 174, 178–180, 185, 189, 205, 228, 247, 248, 266–267, 301–302, 307, 310, 331, 352, 359–361, 389–390, 399, 424–428, 433–437, 440–441, 443–445, 447, 449, 451, *456, 457,* 467, 475, 495–497, 501–502, 505, 518, 536, 545–546, 551

  consolidation, 50, 59, 87, 93, 243, 247–248, 250, 266–268, 358, 361, 490, 550

  multiyear, 10–11, 52, 61–62, 67, 84, 88, 96–97, 128, 148, 177, 205, 251, 325, 348, 367–368, 372, 380, 384, 420, 447 421–422, 434, 447–448

  structure, 7, 9, 50, 129–130, 144, 147, 173, 242–243, 301, 310, 352, 360, *456,* 467, 481–482, 486, 494, 498, 500–502, 505, 518, 541, 549, 556

budgeting, accrual basis, 32, 67–68, 88, 176, 250–251, 366, 372, 389, 547

    capital, 6, 51–54, 67, 85, 92, 128, 146, 148, 185, 187, 199, 244, 267, 308–309, 320, 327, 352–353, 372, 382–383, 386, 424, 467, 492, 495, 547, 561–562, 564

    cash basis, 68, 88, 176, 366–368

    line-item, 9–10, 25, 26, 27, 31, 61, 84, 87, 93, 130, 147, 248, 310, 348, 361–362, 365, 368, 378, 395, 425, 444–445, 547, 556

    major stages in, *13*, 157, 178, 252, 369, 399, 428, 551

    performance, 5, 12, 24, 25, 26–27, 31, 32, 36, 38, 61, 84, 86–87, 89, 93, 101, 143, 175, 192, 223, 249, 260, 310–311, 320, 348, 359–360, 364, 374, 378, 389–390, 425, 437, 439, 448–449, 499, 547, 569

    program, 7–9, 62, 64, 68, 86–87, 89, 96, 133, 147, 310, 320, 360–361, 363, 365, 367, 373, 391, *394*, *457*, 493, 499, 509

    short-term, 66, 105, 127, 251, 331, 350, 467, 523, 543

    techniques, 8–9, (27), 53, 60–61, 67, 86, 88, 133, 147–149, 175, 217it, 248, 270, 310, 320, 348, 360, 361, 363, 365, 367–369, 373, 387–389, 399, 435, 499, 507, 547, 570

    zero-based, 25, 26, 27, 304, 310, 365

cash accounting, 5, 86, 92, 203–204

cash management practices, 5, 46, 56–58, 94, 140, 147, 182–183, 256–257, 265–266, 314, 348, 376–377, 380, 382, *394*, 558

central bank, 57, 558–559, 561

central agencies, *72*, 76, 91, 310, 381

central transfers, conditional, 82–83, 95, 110, 113, 117, 125–126, 129–130, 137, 139–140, 142, 147, 169, 237, 244, 290, 343, 486–487, 496

    unconditional, 82–83, 125, 169, 343, 539

citizen participation, 22, 55, 70, *71*, 108, 134, 146, 150, 159–160, 177, 181, 190, 207, 213, 252, 263–264, 434, 438, *460*, 566

city council, *71*, 133–134, 134, 137–138, 140, 150, 212, 223, 430, 442

commune, 108, 110–112, 114–116, 118–124, 126, 130, 134–140, 143–146, 148, *151–152*, 219–229, 232–239, 242, 244, 246, 247, 252–253, 256–257, 260–264, 266, 269, *271*, 471, 473–474, 476, 481–482, 484, 486–487, 489, 501, 506

contracting out, 95, 312, 382, 446, 456

control, financial, 25, 50, 78, 140–141, 145–146, 163, 168, 179, 181, 183–184, 190, 221, 230–231, 242, 249, 257–259, 265, 270, 280, 282, 312, 315, 380, 441, 475, 495, 500, 506–507, 519, 532, 536, 540, 544, 554, 559–560, 562, 568

    internal, 7, 63, 69–70, 116, 145, 183–184, 265, 342, 245, 259, 265, 316–317, 325, 493, 506–507

debt/debt management, 55, 65, 67, 92, 95, 109, 126, 136, 183–184, 192, 195, 202, 205, 230–232, 241, 245, 253, 256, 264, 266, 334, 338, 349, 354, 372, 380, 382, 384–385, 389, 393, 395, 413, 418, 478, 480, 487, 503, 535, 542, 544, 546, 554

decentralization, 24, 29, 48, 56, 58, 65, 79–80, 92, 107–110, 114, 125–126, 141, 146–149, *151*, 207, 220, 224–225, 260–261, 284, *326*, 343, 376, *396*, 407, 432–433, *450*, *459*, *461*, 469, 471, 482, 511, 516, *517*

decision–making, 5–6, 8–9, 47, 54–55, 65, 78, 81, 91, 110, 150, 206–207, 230, 240, 252, 267, 319–320, 333, 336, 339, 374, 378, 389

effectiveness, 27, 33, 38–39, 48–49, 62, 64, 90–93, 96, 114, 131, 164, 184, 249, 259, 261–262, 268, 287, 312, 317, 334, 336, 372, 374, 378, 381, <u>*394*</u>, 436–437, 439, 445, 447–449, 550, 556, 564, 571

efficiency, 12, 27, 32, 33, 37, 38–39, 49, 62, 117, 135, 140, 149, 164, 184, 187, 189, *211*, 249, 250, 258, 334, 347–248, 356, 360–361, 372, 374, 378, 382, *394*, 416, 426, 429, 431–433, 436–437, 439, 445, 447–449, *460*, 529, 548, 561, 569

expenditures, capital, 6, 12, 48, 67, 85, 87, 131, 137, 168, 187, 197–198, 202, 205, 230, 238–241, 243, 251, 253, 259, 265–267, 291, 292, 295, 333, 352, 367, 372, 408, 424, 481–482, 495–496, 499, 534–536, 546–547

    current, 6, 85, 87, 89, 109, 137, 174, 191, 205, 208, 228–229, 241, 243, 248, 253, 259–260, 262, 265–266, 282, 287, 292, 310, 340–241, 346, 408, 421, 450, 506, 510, 546

extra–budgetary funds, 15, 57, 87, 173, 178, 184, 226, 228, 231, 244, 246–248, 322, 534, 536, 539

fees, local, 81, 123–124, 160, 163, 168–170, 173, 175, 189, 193, 199–200, 202, 210, 226, 264, 287–288, 386, 469–471, 474, 483, 488, 493–494, 496–497, 516, 529–530, 536–538, 545–555, 563–564

finance, local, 92, 117, 129, 137, 147, 149, 160, 164, 167, 181, 187–188, 192, 202–203, 207, 246, 252–254, 257–258, 260, 267, 269, 280, 304, 312, 347, 412, 416, 434, 441, 443–444, *453*, *459–462*, 469–471, 474, 483, 489, 495, 498–500, 509–511, 513–514, 527, 534, 565, 568 forecasting, expenses, 5–6, 11, 97, 130, 136–137, 315, 363, 384, 390, 420, 422

 revenues, 5–6, 130, 136–137, 182, 192, 287, 315, 363, 384, 390,413, 420–422, 429

government, regional, 8, *453*, 527–530, 532–533, 542, 549, 551, 555–556, 564, 567

 sub-national, 79, 82, 278, 334

Gross Domestic Production (GDP), 30, 110, *151*, 200, 231–232, 237, 282, 333, 416, 418, *455*, 468, 478–480

incrementalism, 8, 12, *13*, 27, 35, 87

information systems, 22, 26, 38, 51, 88, 91, 179, 250, 255, 265–266, *272*, 360, 370–371, 375, 389, 391, 421, 467, 503–504, 555

International Monetary Fund, 51, 54, 58, 107, 109, 204, 247, 256, 327, *396*

legislation, 11, 22, 29, 57, 63, 78, 80, 87, 89, 109, 113–114, 129, 132–133, *152*, 172, 183, 192, 197–198, 200, 224, 281, 283–284, 303, 305, 308, 316–317, 322, 334–336, 339, 344, 349–350, 353–354, 361, 367, 372–373, 375, 379–382, 392, *394*, 401–403, 412, 421, 446–448, 469–470, 477, 481, 483, 492–493, 497, 500, 508, 511–512, 516, 525–529, 534–538, 541, 546–547, 549, 553, 558, 561–564, 566–567

line ministry, 117, 125, 138, 346, 475

loan, 10, 50, 83, 115, 129, 170, 184–186, 189, 196, 204, 230, 239, 241, 243, 251, 258, 265, 334, 346–347, 386, 418–419, 421–422, 424, *455*, 486–489, 495–497, 499, 502–503, 505–506, 510–511, 514, 541–542, 545, 548, 553–554, 568, *570*

Ministry of Finance, 30, 36, 50–51, 54, 68–69, 117–118, 126–129, 131, 135–138, 140, 142–144, 146, 163, 174–175, 178–183, 185–186, 188–189, 192, 194–196, 198–200, 202–206, 208–209, *213*, 221, 229–231, 241, 244–245, 248, 252–253, 255–257, 259, 262, 265–266, 269–270, *271*, 279, 287, 292–294, 296–299, 301, 308–313, 321–322, 325, *327*,345, 347, 349, 406, 412,–413, 415, 418–419, 443–445, *455–456, 458–459, 463*, 485, 490, 502, 507, 509, 541, 543, 547, 555, 563–564, 569, *570*

municipal bonds, 186, 470, 487, 512, 514, 542, 561

 company, *72*, 86, 336, 339, 356, 358, 381, 387

 council, 112, 115, 161–164, 172, 175, 177–181, 189–190, 207, 277, 286, 288, 296, 304–307, 315–316, 529–530

new public management, 12, 28, *41*, 88

non–governmental organization (NGO), 6, 86–87, 134, 150, 186, 213, 222, 280–282, 289, 301, 303, 319, *327*

off–budget units (entities), 10, 58–60, 63, 85, 93–94, 132, 148, 246, 310–311, 349, 352, 356–358, 378, 381, 407–411, 440, 444, *453, 455*

output, 26, 27, 31–32, 38–39, 40, 61–62, 64, 69, 84, 88, 176, 303, 348, 360, 364–366, 374, *394*, 416, 425–428, 431–433, 437, 439–440, 442–443, 536

own revenues, 57, 96, 112, 122–123, 133, 142, 168, 170, 186, 192, 202, 237, 246–247, 253, 257, 285–286, 292, 303, 339, 354, 378, 417, 422, *454*, 467, 470, 478, 483, 486–487, 496, 509, 536–537, 562, 565–566

performance indicators, 31, 61, 129, 175–176, 364–365, *395*, 438, 442, 499, 505

 management, 23–25, 29, 92

 measurement, 12, 28, 32–33, *41*, 53, 69, 84, 90–91, 152, 311, 320, 339, 348, 366, 374, *395*, 427, 432, 436, 438–441

Prefect, 49–50, 76, 118, 146, 223, 253, 257, 261, 475–476, 513

prefecture, 118, 138, 143–146, *151, 153*, 513

privatization, 10, 48, 55, 81, 95, 117, 132, 148, 175, 183, 186, 210app, 264, *271–272*, 313, 353, 358, 364, 368, 382, 384, 386, *394*, 408, 416, 430, 469, 478, 518, 536, 538

public enterprise, 10, 34, 87, 235, 247

public investments, 290, 292–294, 314, 325, 407

public service, *41*, 76, 80, 117–118, 122, 124–125, 130, 132, 143, 147–148, 150, 152, 165–166, 168–171, 174, 197, 200, 222, 227–228, 250, 260–261, 263–264, *271*, 278, 283, 333, 338–340, 343, 345, 356–357, 362, 371, 375, *395*, 405,408,411, 416, 419, 421, 431, 434, 445, *456, 461*, 469–471, 473–474, 477–480, 482, 487, 493, 495, 497–498, 506, 511, 516–518, 529, 533

quality, 6–7, 24, 27, 29, 34, 38, 41, 62, 64–65, *71*, 132, 139, 149, 180, 187, 189, 191, 207, 225, 245, 249–250, 268–269, 312, 324, 365–366, 374–375, 383, 416, 421, 425–426, 428, 431–433, 435, 437–439, 443, 445, 448, 451, 482, 489, 516, 564

region, 109–112, 115–116, 119, 121–122, 124, 126–127, 136, 138, 140, 144, *151*, 162, *208*, 220, 253, 262, 269, 278–279, 333, 342, 375, 403, 406–408, 410, 412–413, 493, *517*, 525–530, 534, 540–541, 547–548, 560, 562, 564–566, *570*

regulation, economic, 79, 171–172, 224, 238, 246, 259, 269, *272*, 475, 509, 512, 514, *518*, 561–562, 564

 legal, 108, 120, 126, 141, 144, 149, 160, 162, 164, 224, 278, 288, 333–334, 338–339, 348, 351, 360, 473, 506, 525–526, 563

reporting, 31, 37, 51, 53–54, 58, 60, 62–63, 65, 68, 70, 86, 89, 91, 135, 144–145, 147, 174–175, 179, 181, 184, 189, 203, 221, 241, 243, 249–252, 254–257, 259, 262, 265–266, 269, *272*, 297, 299, 310, 325, 334, 366, 370–372, 378, 389, 429, 440, 442–443, 445, 451, *460*, 505, 530, 544, 560, 568

State Budget Expenditures, 110, 126

strategic planning, 38, 127, 172, 242, 300, 350, 374, 544

subsidy, 27, 65, 68–69, 131, 163, 167–169, 171–174, 178–180, 182, 185–189, 192–196, 199–202, 204, 206, *208–209*, 293, 318, 323, 340–341, 346, 357–358, *393*, 414–415, 417, 452, 454, *456*, 469–470, 475, 478, 481–482, 485, 487–489, 495–499, 517, 536–537, 539–541, 546, 549–551, 564

tax, local, 50, 83, 108, 115, 117–118, 123–124, 126, 140, 147, 160, 168–170, 173, 175, 182–183, 189, 189, 193, 199–200, 207, *210*, 232, 233–234, 262–263, 280, 285–287, 342–346, 353, 355, 364, 367, 384, 386–387, 421, 469–471, 474, 483, 488, 493–494, 496, 516, 525, 527–530, 536–537, 541, 561, 563–566

    policy, 25, 49, 336, 375, 483, 493, 514–516, 543, 567, 537, 539, 562

    shared, 65, 125–126, 168–169, 173, 182, 192–196, 199–202, 206, *209*, 233–234, 263, 290, 320, 346, *393*, 405, 412–415, 417, 470, 485–488, 494, 508–511, 513, 537, 541

transparency, 11–12, 39, 58–59, 69, 86, 148, 164, 200, 237, 249, 312–313, 348, 354, 356, 361, 388, 436, 447, *455*, 566

treasury, central, 77, 114, state 348–349, 475, 488–489, 491–492, 495, 506, 512, 514, 559–561

    system, 60, 68, 92, 132, 142, 221, 254, 256, 265–266, *272*, 279, 287, 299–300, 314, 376, 391, 458, 558

user charges, 96, 124, 169, 235, 289, 281, 345, 385, 537–538

World Bank, 54, 58, 88, 107, 109, 239, *327*, 348, 388, *395–396*, 459, 460, 489, 496